Oct.

Sonya

YOUR *Life*
IS YOUR
Journey

I pray my book
touches your life!
many blessings to you!
God bless you

Jennifer Lupone

JENNIFER LUPONE

ISBN 978-1-63961-600-8 (paperback)
ISBN 978-1-63961-601-5 (digital)

Christian Faith Publishing
832 Park Avenue
Meadville, PA 16335
www.christianfaithpublishing.com

Printed in the United States of America

For starters, I'd like to thank God for all he has done in my life. If it weren't for him, it would not be possible for this book to get published. He is the reason why I can do all great things. Thanks be to God for leading me to in a great church called Cornerstone. It is located in Oxford, Connecticut. My faith has grown in more ways than one by going here.

A big thank-you goes out to everyone at Christian Faith Publishing Company for all their hard work and dedication for getting this done. Thank you for giving me this opportunity to be an author as well.

I would also like to include some important people in my life:

My aunt Grace. She was my mom's sister and has been like a mom to me since my mom went to be with the Lord.

My cousin, Tina, who is more like my sister, and her boyfriend Billy

My sister, Jody, and my brother-in-law, Craig.

My brother, John, and sister-in-law, Michelle.

My uncle Danny and his caregiver, Jicela.

My boyfriend Bobby and family

My niece, Sarah, and her fiancé, Eric, and my two great nephews Brody and Mason.

My nephew Kevin and his girlfriend, Krystal.

I just want to give you all a big thank you for being part of my life. I'm grateful, thankful, and blessed that you are all in my life. You all make it complete. You are all always in my prayers. Amen.

To My uncle/dad who passed away in March of 2016. He was like my dad pretty much all of my life. He was my aunt Grace's partner in crime. I dedicate this book to him because he gave me the push to pursue writing. May you be resting in heaven.

To my mom and all my loved ones who passed on, I love and miss you all.

To all my friends, thank you so much for being in my life. Thank you for your love, encouragement, and support. You are always in my prayers.

To my coworker crew at Cost Cutters Hair Salon located on 100 Main St N Southbury, Connecticut, I love working with all of you. I feel we have a great team. I love you, girls!

Contents

Preface

Sometimes life throws us curves. We feel like giving up, and we think things will never get better. My intention for writing this book is to be able to lift up the lives of many. I want to be able to show and help people that they don't have to live life in fear, to be anxious, depressed, bitter, angry, to have regrets, and more. God doesn't give us anything that we can't handle.

Things may not seem like they will work out; but in the end, they will.

I love to write because it sets me apart from the world. Writing helps me figure out my own problems. It opens up my mind to so much beauty and sets my mind free to imagination. It is one of the things that comes natural to me. My uncle, who was like a dad to me, passed away five years ago. He always said I should pursue writing. This book is dedicated to him.

As we know, life happens; and we all get caught up with living the busy life. To me though, it doesn't matter how long it takes for us to achieve our goals and dreams. There is no deadline. We all live different lives and have different shoes to fill; so with that, I say run your own race and continue to climb that mountain. Nothing is ever impossible. God has a plan for us all. Talk to him, and he will lead you on the right path. I live in faith.

I hope my book touches many lives. I feel like the title says it all, *Your Life Is Your Journey*—meaning, we all go through trials in our life, whether they are good or bad. We are living our life's journey. This is not my autobiography, so I will not be writing my life events in the order that my life took place. This book was meant to help others to know they are not alone. I was in a dark place in my life at one point as I'm sure we all have been or still are. Every chapter has its own unique story, just like every human being. We all have our own story to tell. May my book touch your heart and open your world to new things. Get ready to live your life's journey.

Chapter 1

LEARNING TO LIVE LIFE HAPPY

So many times, we compare ourselves to others, whether it be what one has or that someone else's life is better than our own. Instead of wishing we had what the other has, we shall be grateful for what we do have and for the life God has given us. This is something I've always lived by, and that is to run your own race. Be the best version of yourself. Don't compare yourself to others. If you do, you will just be making yourself miserable, and it will be that much harder for you to succeed. In the following paragraphs, I will list ways in which you can live life with a grateful heart.

Every morning when you awake, thank God for giving you another day to make it better than yesterday. Write down on a piece of paper all the great things you have in your life, and put it where you will read it daily. Read something encouraging and inspiring daily. This can be something as simple as a devotional book, a favorite quote, or a motivational book—the Bible. Writing in a journal daily will help you as well. It will help clear your mind of things that may have upset you or even made you mad. As you write in your journal about these things, it will help you have a better day tomorrow.

In order to live a happy life, you have to be happy with your inner self. Nobody can make you happy. You must learn to love the person God created you to be. A few ways you can learn to be happy with yourself is to write down on a piece of paper your best qualities, things you are good at, things that make you unique from others, things that people may tell you what you are good at. Write down the compliments people may give you. Look in the mirror daily, and tell yourself you are awesome, beautiful, talented, courageous, smart, and may the rest of the list that you say about yourself remain positive.

I was not always so positive and happy within my inner self; but as I got older, this changed. You see, as we get older, we tend not to care what people think and say about us. I would care about what people thought and said about me. Well I was also shy when I was younger, so that did not help with my insecurities that I had inside of me. As we get older, we mature and get wiser. So that is how I got over being shy and not caring of what people thought and said about me. It did not happen overnight; but what does?

It takes time for us to mature and for things to change within our inner selves. How I overcame my shyness was by working at Dunkin' Donuts at the age of nineteen. The year I worked at Dunkin' Donuts was 1995. I worked there for seven years. I became the assistant manager after two years of working there. Being around people helps break you out of your shell. It helped me be more outgoing.

Reflecting back to my other jobs before Dunkin' Donuts, I helped work a family business at the age of twelve. I didn't get paid, but I did get an allowance for helping out. The business was my uncle Joe's business. By the way, he is my uncle who was like my dad, who I dedicated this book to and who passed away five years ago. He had his own ice cream business called Humpty Dumpty. His father passed down the business to him. It was an old ice-cream truck he sold off of. It was actually an awesome antique ice-cream truck that had an antique ice-cream trailer that we would hook up to it. I remember helping to paint it.

My cousin Tina, Mom, Aunt Grace—who by the way was my uncle's better half—helped with working the family business too. We would sell the ice cream at Kent Falls State Park in the town called Kent in Connecticut. A few years later came an addition to the business: a hotdog cart.

You see, my uncle would leave the ice-cream trailer there for us to sell out of to the customers while he went around Kent and other parks and campgrounds to sell ice cream.

Years later, while my uncle Joe was selling ice cream in Kent, he ran into someone who needed help with tube rentals. People would rent out the tubes to go floating down the river. So my uncle had asked me if I would be interested in working there. I said yes. It was $10 under the table, and I was so happy to be making money. It was a fun summer job.

As I sit and write my book, I reflect back at some of my other insecurities that I had growing up. Getting picked on in high school and coming home every day crying was no fun. It made me feel awful about myself. I felt like there was something wrong with me. I would be in class or walking down the hallway and get called names. I felt like crawling in a whole and never coming out. I was nice to everyone, so why was I the one getting picked on? It made me upset and hurt. Well you see kids are cruel. Bullying should be stopped. If you are from a small town like Oxford, like I was, and not from a rich town like Monroe, then you were not going to fit in. I also felt like I didn't fit in because my mom could only afford to buy me clothes at consignment stores. Plus, I was shy back then. I am against bullying; so when I hear or see kids getting bullied, I will stick up for them.

As I reflect back and to now, though, I realize it is not about how many friends we have; it is who remains in our lives through the good, and not so good times, that matters.

It was the second year of that high school that I was going to try and attempt another year, but I still got harassed and picked on. Then my aunt stepped in and told my mom she can not go through another year like this again. My mom loved that school because of the education but then agreed with my aunt. My mom taught me how to stick up for myself, but it was not going to happen in that school.

Looking back and to now, I do have regrets that I didn't stand my ground. I wish I hadn't let those kids chase me out of that school. If I could go back in time, I would have done things differently. I was scared back then to stand my ground though. If you are going through something like this, stand your ground. Don't allow anyone to bully you and make you feel like you don't belong. I'm not the same person I was in high school.

This is something I live by: With age brings wisdom. With weakness brings strength to be stronger.

I feel that all schools should have a teaching class on how not to bully others and how to get along with others. You know, like a class they have daily, like they have for math, english, gym, etc. This way, maybe it would prevent suicides, violence, and so forth from happening.

So off to Seymour High School, I went that year of 1992. My cousin also attended Seymour High School.

She was a year behind me. I did have some problems at that school, but my cousin Tina, who is more like a sister to me, stood up for me, and that was that. There was no more picking on me.

Even though I was not getting picked on, I still felt like I did not belong. I had no luck with getting a boyfriend when I was younger. This made me feel ugly inside and out. Being shy and not being outgoing did not help with my insecurities that I was feeling inside.

Reflecting back, I realize I was not the problem; but they were. As the years went by, this all made me stronger. I felt more secure within myself. I choose not to care about what people say and think about me. With my strong faith, I now realize the only person that I have to ever answer to is God. He is the maker and our father who is awesome. At the end of the day, you must be happy with yourself and your accomplishments. In order to be loved, you must learn to love yourself. I was a work in progress. I got through it with God's help. If you feel like I did then, you just gotta believe and talk to God because he will help get you through all the bad times. He will see to it that what comes around goes around.

In order to live an extraordinary life, you have to put things into motion and perspective. Every day you awake, thank God for a new day to make changes, eat right, exercise, read, or listen to personal development. This could be anything from the Bible, a book that talks about how to grow, and be a better you. It can be listening to something encouraging on a CD that will help get you on the right path in life. Do whatever it takes for you to live every day with a grateful heart. As we know, life is not long enough to live it unhappy.

Other ways to help you live an extraordinary life is to set your mind to goals and work on them every day. Don't just dream about them, but turn them into reality. Write them down on paper, and reflect back on them daily. This will help keep you focused. Listening to others' negativity won't get you far in your life's journey. You have to learn to block out negativity. Naysayers will try to put you down because they aren't happy with their own lives or with themselves. If you listen to what others are saying about you, it will hold you back from succeeding. When people talk negatively to you, the best thing you can do for yourself is look at yourself in the mirror and say what they are saying is not true because I'm a child of God who wants me to do great things in my life's journey.

Life, as we know, is not always easy; but if we give up, then we never see what the outcome will be. God never promised us a rose garden, but what he did promise us is that he will always be by our side every step of the way. He paid for our sins, so now it is our turn to pay it forward by making our lives better and for us to help one another. If we give more and expect little in return, we will feel better about who we are.

Life is not always getting what we want. If something is not going our way, we tend to get bitter and angry. This is no way to live. When something doesn't go our way, we have to learn to live through it and make it better. Try and come up with a better solution to make it better. Think positive, and talk yourself through the bad times. Things don't always go as planned so you have to be ready when things do not go right. Getting mad, angry, and upset won't help the situation. It is too much work to get this way. The way we handle things isn't always the best way, but we tend to grow and learn from every given situation. After all, nothing is perfect.

I will give you an example of what happened to me when my plans got interrupted. You see, my boyfriend at the time and I never seemed to have gotten a chance to spend the whole day together, so I was looking forward to spending the whole day with him. But life, as we know, happens. Well he ended up having to work. I was not happy. I was not angry with him; I was just not happy about the situation. I let the situation get in the way of me being in a great mood.

I was working two jobs at the time. I was a hairstylist and a certified nurse aide. He was a truck driver, so you can see where the frustration came in with not being able to spend much time together.

When I think back, I've learned from it. I have learned to handle it differently. Instead of getting mad and upset, I said to myself, there is nothing I can do about it. It is not his fault he had to work. Besides, he did not have to work all day. We still got to spend time together. You see, we tend to stress about things we cannot control. We tend to stress out sometimes for nothing because in the end things work out. This is when walking in faith and not by sight comes in.

Walking in faith and not by sight means that we can't see what's going to happen until it happens, so we need to remain in faith. I know this is not always easy. Believe me, I get it; but we gotta start somewhere, right?

When we let go of our fears and stop negativity from happening, the better we will be able to live our lives. We will become happier individuals. I know this isn't always possible; but if we program our minds to do this, the better at it we will become when difficult situations arise. We cannot change what we cannot change. The only thing we can do is live our lives to the fullest and worry less. Unfortunately, worrying won't keep the bad stuff from happening.

When we are happy within our inner selves, we can be grateful for what we have, we can be happy with the life we are given and we can love ourselves.

In God's eyes, we are enough, and we matter. So with that in mind, never give up on being the best version of yourself.

Some of us tend to want people to like us. We feel that the more friends we have, the happier we will feel and be. Because of this, we will go as far as putting other people's happiness ahead of our own. If we are not careful, people will take advantage of our kindness and our generosity. Like I said earlier, as we get older, we realize it is not important how many friends we have. We tend to realize who our friends are. So with that being said, open your heart to who your friends are and not the ones who will take advantage of your kindness and generosity.

Sometimes we look for the approval of others. Keep this in mind, we do not need approval from anyone because God already approves us. To feel this, you must search within your inner self. Pray about it. Pray for God to lead the way, and he will. Write down on paper your best qualities. Write down what you need to work on about yourself. This will help gain you the confidence you need.

We do not need to be forgiven by another soul. So if you are waiting, stop. God already forgave us for our sins. Learn to find forgiveness within yourself. If people want to hold grudges, then that's on them. Holding grudges just takes away our happiness. When we let go of bitterness, our soul is happy; and so is God. Nobody is perfect, and we all make mistakes. How I have learned to find forgiveness was to pray about it.

Life, as we know, doesn't go as planned. Like I said, worrying won't stop the bad stuff from happening. Life will happen. The bad things will happen; so hold on to the good things that come along. Try and embrace the bad things when they do happen, and try to be prepared when they do arise.

When you are feeling stressed and worried, these five things will help you along:

1. Take a deep breath; inhale and exhale. (Do that for about five minutes or longer if you need to.)
2. Take a brisk walk daily; exercise at least three to five times a week.
3. Meditate for ten minutes daily. Examples of what you can do to meditate are listening to soft music, like water sounds, or by being in a room by yourself with your eyes closed and just relaxing with your mind clear of worry. There are lots of apps on phones, tablets, etc. to help you meditate as well.
4. Read something inspiring and uplifting.
5. Drink plenty of water.

There are apps on our phones that can help us keep track of our water intake as well. The app that I have is called Drink Water Reminder. It is great because it calculates how much water you should be drinking daily. All you have to do is put in your weight, and it shows you how much to drink.

To conclude this chapter, take time out of your busy day, and do something you enjoy doing. When we do these things regularly, they will become a habit in our daily lives.

Chapter 2

FEELING FEARLESS

Wherever you are in your life, just know it is never too late to try new things. It doesn't matter how old you are. After all, age has no impact on your well-being, and it is just a number.

Have you ever heard the saying "nothing is impossible"? Well the word alone says you are possible and can do the impossible—I'm possible. See, I told you.

Sometimes, in order to find ourselves, it is good to be alone. This way, we can figure out what we want out of our life. We can stay focused on our goals, career, and such. We can also really search our inner selves and take time to find out who we truly are as a person. This also helps us get on the right path in life that God has set forth for us. We can also get better connected with God.

When we get out of our own way, we realize we are enough. We are able to get out of our comfort zone, and that is when the magic happens. When we try new things and they don't work out for us, it does not mean that we failed. It just means that it wasn't for us, and it wasn't meant to be. If something is bringing more stress than passion and happiness, then it is time to cut the cord.

I once was a Mary Kay consultant. I love the products, company, and what it stands for; but it was not for me. I mean I enjoyed doing it, but it caused me too much anxiety and stress. It was not bringing me happiness. I was getting stressed and overwhelmed with not getting the parties, not making money, and not being able to have the time to invest in doing it.

With me, I have to be able to put my all into something. I guess if I wanted it bad enough, I would have tried harder. That goes with anything though. If you want something bad enough, you will do whatever it takes to succeed. That is why I say, when something doesn't work out, you can't say you failed at it. I don't look at it that I failed at Mary Kay. In fact, I look at it as a learning lesson. If we don't try things, then how do we know if it is for us or not? There are so many successful consultants that do awesome with the company. I would *never ever* tell someone not to be a Mary Kay consultant or not to do anything for that matter. If anything, I would encourage them to do it and be supportive. I love seeing others succeed and do great. I live to inspire. This is one of the many reasons why I wrote this book.

When things don't work out and go as planned, we have to keep on moving forward. Over analyzing the situation will just make it worse. When we try new things, and they do not work out, it's called living and feeling fearless while we are doing it. The word fearless to me is someone who is willing to take chances. If we do not take the leap of faith, then we will never know what the outcome will be. Besides, God made us to be more than average.

At one time, I was working two jobs and trying to work Mary Kay in the mix of it all. I was and still am working as a hairstylist, but I was also working at Visiting Nurse Services as a CNA (certified nurses aid). It was rough working fifty to sixty hours a week between both jobs and sometimes not getting a day off for two weeks then trying to fit Mary Kay in. I mean, there are people who can manage to do all that and more. But we are all different, so we can't compare ourselves to others. We all live our lives differently and have more obligations and responsibilities.

I knew for me I had to make changes because the life I was living was not bringing me happiness. It was causing me stress with trying to work the two jobs, trying to find time to do Mary Kay, and so forth. I can't speak for everyone, but as for me, money isn't everything. I mean, what good is it if we don't have our sanity? God did not design our lives for us to always be busy. Busy running here. Busy running there. This is not a healthy way to live. He didn't design our lives to be so busy that we forget to just live, relax, be laid back, and more. He didn't design our lives so that we would be so busy that we couldn't enjoy the life we are given. He designed our lives so we can live it happily and not so stressful.

We must enjoy the life we are given, embrace the good and the not so good, because as we know, things can change in a blink of an eye.

I do believe it's better to take a risk than to miss a moment of magic. Run your own race, and don't compare yourself with anyone else. Look ahead and not what anyone else is doing. We all accomplish our goals at different speeds. It doesn't matter how fast we get to where we are going as long as we accomplish our goals. After all, we have our own life's journey to fulfill. Be happy with yourself and your success. Always challenge yourself. Be the best version of yourself. Listen to God, for he knows your destiny and what's best for you.

One day, I decided to take the leap of faith and quit being a certified nurse aide. I love being a hairstylist. I believe it is my calling. It is my passion. I don't look at it as a job. It's something I enjoy doing. When you love what you do, it doesn't feel like work. I decided to quit being a CNA so I could have more time to pursue my hairdressing career and Mary Kay. If it wasn't for me giving Mary Kay a go, then I'd still be doing both jobs; and I wouldn't know where it would take me. I most likely would have regrets as well. You see, things work out in the end.

Sometimes it's hard to see the light at the end of the tunnel. That is why we have to walk in faith and not by sight. Ask God to lead us in the path he has set out for us. He already knows what our destiny and our life's journey looks like. It is all laid out for us. It's like us watching a movie/TV show we've already seen before. We already know what's going to happen, right? Well that's the same thing with God. You see, God already knows what is going to happen in our lives before we even know what's going to happen. This is why it is so important to draw ourselves closer to him. Let God in our lives; and I promise you, it will be better. God is helping me write this book for sure. He is guiding me on what to say. Amen to that!

Some people won't agree with the decisions we make, and that's okay. It isn't their life, nor is it their business. If there is anything I've learned, it would be that I don't need approval from others. The quicker people start to live like this, the happier they'll be.

I know people say that we all are given the same twenty-four hours in a day and that if they have time to do things, then so can everyone else. Well guess what, we may be given the same twenty-four hours, but we all live different lives. We all have different situations that are going on in our lives. And furthermore, we are all different from one another. Stop beating yourself up about it. Like I said, concentrate on yourself and not what others are doing. Some people are better at managing their time, so they are able to get more things done on a given day; and some just have to learn to manage their time more. Don't worry, I have this problem too.

Don't just dream your dreams, but live them. When we search within our souls, we will find that we can master our goals and succeed. When this happens, the life we are living becomes fearless. It is kind of like the ocean. It is dark and spooky at night; but when it is daylight, it is not so scary. Do you see the metaphor here? In order to be fearless, we have to get out of the darkness so that the fog can be lifted away. If we remain in the darkness, then we will never find our way to the top, and we will stay stuck in the same place we are a year from today. If we continue to live our lives in solitude, then we will always feel alone. In the next paragraph, I will help you in some ways to not feel this way.

There are many things you can do to help you not feel scared or alone. Here are some ideas for you: Go to church. Go to church gatherings. Be around other Christians who will help bring out the best in you. Find friends who will lift you up rather than tear you apart. Go to social gatherings. Join groups that will help get you out of your shell. Avoid negative people and people who are not for you. Avoid jealous people and naysayers. People like this will only bring you down, and it won't be good for your overall well-being. Life isn't long enough for any of this. Try exercising as this is great for our whole well-being.

There are a few scriptures in the Bible that I love that talks about this too. They definitely speak to me as I'm writing my book.

Second Timothy 1:7: Be strong like that, because God has given us his spirit. And his spirit does not cause us to be afraid. Instead, he causes us to be strong to serve God. He helps us to love God and other people, and he helps us to rule ourselves properly.

Philippians 4:6: Do not worry about anything. Instead, pray to God about everything. Ask him to help you with things that you need and thank him for his help.

Philippians 4:7: If you do that, God will give you peace in your minds. That peace is so great that nobody can completely understand it. You will not worry or be afraid because you belong to Christ Jesus.

Psalms 34:4: I asked the Lord to help me, and he answered me. He saved me from everything that made me afraid.

Psalms 56:3: Most high God, when I am afraid, I will trust in you.

One more example is Joshua 1:9: Remember that I have told you to do this. So be strong and do not be afraid. Do not be weak but be brave. I, the Lord your God, will be with you, everywhere that you go.

I read the Bible daily, so I pray that these scriptures that I share with you helps because they help me.

There is nothing wrong with having alone time. In fact, it is healthy and brings you clarity. I know this to be true because I do it, and it feels awesome. Meditation, taking a walk, reading, listening to calm sounds are all great ways to spend your time alone. There's an excellent app called Calm you can download on your tablet and phone. Try it because your soul will feel happy and at ease.

While it is okay to be alone sometimes, it is not healthy to always want to be alone. It is not healthy because that is how depression will work its way into our soul. It is easy to get caught up with being alone and wanting to be alone; but if we are not careful, it'll eat us up inside and cause a life of loneliness, misery, health problems, and more.

When we've been hurt by others, it's easy to want to shut the world out and put the walls up; but this is not healthy. I've done this myself.

People would hurt me. So to prevent someone else from hurting me, I would put the walls up. It is an awful thing not being able to trust when we get hurt; but that's when God, our maker, comes in. He will help us when we turn to him for answers. He will show us how to trust and remove people from our lives that are not bringing us the gift he gave us; and that is happiness. Besides God and my faith, here are a few scriptures that I turn to in times that helped me knock down the walls and how to trust:

Proverbs 3:5: Always trust the Lord completely. Do not think your own wisdom is good enough.

Luke 16:10: If you can trust a person with a very small thing, you can also *trust* him with bigger things. And if you cannot trust a person with a very small thing, then you cannot trust him with a big thing.

Colossians 3:13: Do not become angry with each other. If you think that someone has done something wrong against you, forgive them. Remember that the Lord has forgiven you, so you should also forgive other people. When someone has done you wrong, do not seek revenge. Instead, walk away from the situation, and be the better person. God will take care of it all. Remember this for all the times we get mad, feel bitter, hold grudges, and so forth. It takes time away from us living a happy life. Life, as we know it, isn't long enough to live it unhappy.

Here are a few encouraging thoughts that I choose to live by myself: Caring is free, so go out and share it with the world. Being fearless is free, so go on and live it. Be bold, daring, courageous, spontaneous; be who you were born to be. Don't surrender because your next opportunity might be your next big thing. Beauty happens inside our souls. As we know, looks grow old. Let your love shine through from the inside out, and always be the best version of yourself. Amen.

When people aren't feeling good about themselves and aren't happy with their own lives, they tend to want to make others miserable. People like this will try to belittle you; but don't let them win. Ever heard "misery loves company"? Well these are the people that cause it for you. Do yourself a favor, and go the other way. If you are like me, I tend to see the good in others; and I want to give people the benefit of the doubt. Sometimes I don't go with my first instincts, which I really should. I do believe in giving second chances because nobody is perfect. That's why they make erasers.

When I am double-crossed, I move on and pray for people that double-cross me because revenge is a waste of time. Revenge is crippling to our soul. Besides, I don't have time for it. I have to write this book. Well even if I wasn't writing this book, it would still be a waste of my time. When people say mean, hurtful, or bad things behind our back or even to our faces, ignore them and walk away. Don't even respond to this behavior. I know it won't be easy because I'm still working on this myself, but it is something we have to work on. Give it to the Lord.

When we look deep inside our souls, we will find what people say about us isn't true. We are children of God. He made us and loves us regardless of what others say. Every morning, we shall look in the mirror and say to ourselves, "I am awesome. I'm not going to eat the bad fruit of negativity. I'm going to eat the good fruit of positivity. No matter what kind of day I'm going to have, God has my back." Let this be a routine you do daily, and the seeds of God will blossom into your soul. God loves this talk, but the enemy does not. The enemy wants us to live life hating ourselves and others.

When this happens, say, "Not today, devil, not today," and repeat what I said in the paragraph of what to do daily.

I use this weapon—the blood of Jesus or the Holy Spirit— because the enemy doesn't like it. It does work. We need to understand that the only way you can overcome Satan in this day and age is through the blood of Jesus Christ. Satan fears Calvary. You put your sin under the blood of Jesus Christ. The Bible says the blood of Jesus Christ, God's Son, cleanses us from all sin. Satan fears the blood of Christ. Be saved through the shed blood of the Lord Jesus Christ. Come to Him and say, "Oh, Father, in my hand, no price I bring, simply to thy cross I cling." Satan says, "Oh no! He has come by the way of the cross! Oh no, I wish he had not done that. They overcome him by the blood of the Lamb." When we say the Holy Spirit, hear what it says here: There are a number of contrasts that the Bible gives between Satan and the Holy Spirit—the Third Person of the Trinity. Satan is the serpent, while the Holy Spirit is the dove. The Holy Spirit is the Spirit of truth, while Satan is a liar. The Holy Spirit searches the deep things of God, while Satan also has his deep things. The Holy Spirit is a life-giving Spirit, while Satan is a murderer. Satan is the slanderer of God's people, while the Holy Spirit is the Advocate of the believer. Wow, now that is powerful, isn't it? So when the enemy tries to put ideas in your head of things that are *not* happening, shout out the Holy Spirit or the blood of Jesus! Amen and woo-hoo to that!

If something or someone is not bringing you happiness, then let it go. Let them go, and move on. You have more important things to focus on in your life's journey. The mountain you are climbing may seem hard at first. It may seem impossible. You may even feel like giving up; but don't. You will be happy with yourself because you didn't let defeat get in your way. If we look at what is in front of us rather than what is ahead of us, then it won't seem impossible. Instead, it will become possible. Keep on living a fearless life. Keep on living in your positive circle. Let that positive magnet that surrounds you help keep the negative out. Lastly, let your faith take over everything.

Chapter 3

WHEN YOUR HEART BREAKS—MENTAL/ PHYSICAL ABUSE

We've all had our hearts broken, I'm sure. Some of us have had our share of broken hearts. Whether it be from a death, a relationship, or something else. We may feel like our lives are over or that we will never move on from it, but we do. We also tend to hold back when we get hurt. We have fear of rejection, uncertainty, betrayal, and maybe more. When our heart gets broken it is hard to trust again. We get close to people and then back away because we feel insecure. It feels like a repeated pattern that will never seem to end. We put up walls because we are afraid to let others in. This reflects back to chapter 2 when I talked about this. It may seem like I'm repeating myself, but I just want to reflect back on a little that I've talked about already. If we keep doing this, our life will be harder, sadder, and more.

As time goes on, we realize that the pain we were once feeling makes us a stronger and better person. Everything we go through in life makes us who we are. Our past doesn't define who we are. We learn from our past mistakes, reflect back, and move forward from our past. It's all a part of growing. Our strength comes from our Lord and within our souls.

Death is not an easy thing to go through. We feel that life will never be able to go on again. Our emotions run high. We can't think straight. Our hearts are broken in two. I know this all too well. My mom entered heaven on October 30, 1994. She was only fifty-three when she passed away. She had a heart attack. I was in my senior year of high school. I just turned nineteen three days before she passed away. That was the worst night of my life.

We were very close. I felt like I could tell my mom anything, and she would never tell another soul. I get that from her, along with many other awesome traits too. I look exactly like her too. My family tells me that as well, and it makes me feel good and happy. My mom was the best. She had a great, big heart and would do anything for anyone. Her soul definitely lives on. I feel her presence all the time. She is my guardian angel for sure. Even though it has been twenty-six years that my mom hasn't physically been here on earth, I still miss her just as if she passed away yesterday, if not more.

Although my mom passed at a young age, she has a sister, who is my aunt, and she has been like a mom to me. My aunt Grace is my aunt, who I have mentioned in chapter 1. She is my aunt who told my mom that she needed to get me out of Masuk High School. I talked about how we all worked the family ice cream business as well. My aunt Grace's husband, who is my uncle, has been like a dad to me too. He passed away five years ago. That was another heartbreak and felt like a nightmare. He went in to have an aortic aneurysm repair done at the veterans' hospital but didn't make it. We tried to talk him into having it done elsewhere, but he was old-school and wanted it done there. We believe the doctor messed up; but without really hard evidence, it was a hard case to prove. You see, my uncle's surgery was a scheduled case. We walked in with him and walked out without him. When I say it felt like a nightmare on what went on at the VA that day, it really did. It felt like something you would see in a movie and not in real life. They never kept us informed on how his surgery was going. They operated on his lungs, because supposedly, he had blebs on his lungs. I feel it was a cover-up, because in his medical records, it stated that there was a tear in his lung. Well, you don't just get a tear in the lung unless it was punctured. They never came out and told us that they were operating on his lungs either. We should have been informed what was going on. The doctor left the VA around 9:00 p.m. and then came back all decked out and in high heels. We were like, "What the heck is going on?" We were there from 6:00 a.m. until 7:00 a.m. the next morning. It was a heartbreak. Like I've said, malpractice is a hard case to prove. My cousin Tina talked to lawyers and couldn't get anywhere. By the way, my uncle Joe was my cousin Tina's dad, and her mom is my aunt Grace.

I wish I could have a redo of that whole day, but as we know, we can't change what has already been done. We don't have the answers as to why bad things happen. Someday we will know, but while we are on this earth, we must trust God's plans for us.

It isn't easy when our loved ones pass on; but having a strong faith is what does get us through. How I cope is knowing that they would not want us to be sad. They would want us to carry on with our lives and live our life's journey happy. We still have our lives to live, and we can either choose to live it bitterly, angrily, making everyone else around us unhappy; or we can choose to make it better. Our loved ones do not want us to be miserable. They are still around us and watching over us, so it is important to let them see us happy and living our best life.

We never get over missing and having our loved ones physically around us, we just learn to cope with it. I'm not saying I never have hard days of not missing my loved ones because I do. The memories are always there. I can feel my loved ones are close by. You see, when our faith is strong, then we can go on. We all have our own beliefs; but I feel that having a strong mindset, praying, and more help us cope better. God is always there to help us through the good and bad days as well.

In the next paragraph, I'm going to share with you some scriptures. I hope you enjoy them as much as I do; and may they help you like they've helped me.

Ephesians 6:10: At the end of my letter, I want to say this to you: Be united with the Lord so that you are strong. Then his great power will help you.

Hosea 13:14: I will redeem these people. People will not have to bury them. I will redeem them from death. Death, your illnesses, have gone. Death cannot kill any longer.

Psalms 23:4: I may walk through a valley that is dark as death. But I will not be afraid of any danger. This is because you are with me, Lord. Your stick and shepherd's pole make me feel brave.

Romans 10:9: The message is this: You must say clearly that Jesus is the Lord. Also, you must believe deep inside yourself that God raised him to life again after his death. Then God will save you.

In the next paragraphs, I will be talking about going through breakups and letting go from them.

Going through a breakup isn't easy; but when we are away from the situation we were once in, we tend to see things clearer. We know what we want out of the relationship and what we don't want. Sometimes, no matter how much we try to make things work, some things aren't meant to be. Nobody should ever put up with anybody's abusive behavior. That means physically and mentally.

In the next paragraphs, I'm going to talk more about what exactly abusive behavior is. You may know someone who needs help and doesn't know how to seek the help they need in order to live a more stable, healthier life. I know it is not the most inspiring thing to talk about, but some of us go through this in our life's journey. I believe it could be helpful for others to know about it.

What is physical abuse? Physical abuse in a relationship often starts gradually, such as with a push or a slap, and then becomes progressively worse over time. Physical violence is always illegal. If you feel afraid of your partner all of the time, you steer clear of certain topics to avoid making your partner angry. You feel like you can't do anything right. You are walking on eggshells because of their anger and rage. Physical abuse involves a person using physical force against you, which causes, or can cause, you harm.

Physical abuse can involve any of the following violent acts: scratching or biting, pushing or shoving, slapping, kicking, choking or strangling, throwing things, force-feeding or denying you food, using weapons or objects that can hurt you, physically restraining you (such as pinning you against a wall, floor, bed, etc.), reckless driving, other acts that hurt or threaten you.

How it starts

Many survivors of physical abuse say that the violence started with just a slap or a push but then became more intense over time.

Blaming you. An abuser will often blame someone else, such as the victim, for saying or doing something that "caused" their violent behavior. Or they might say their behavior was a result of being under the influence of alcohol or drugs or feeling stressed or frustrated.

Telling you they're sorry. It's also quite common for the abuser to feel remorse and to apologize after an assault. They may beg for forgiveness and promise they'll never do it again. They will quite often sincerely regret what they've done, which makes it more difficult for the victim of the assault to leave the relationship.

What you need to remember. Their violent behavior is always their responsibility and not yours. Abuse is never okay or justifiable. Whatever they say, their violence is never acceptable.

What should you do if you've been physically abused? If you've experienced physical abuse, it's essential that you seek help. There are a number of services that can offer support. Most importantly, if you're currently fearful or you believe you're in danger, immediately call 911.

Another tool that can help you is downloading the Emergency Plus app. This app (https://emergencyapp.triplezero.gov.au) can help you if you don't know your exact location when you call Triple Zero (000). The app uses the GPS on your smartphone to give you a location address where available. Or you can use what3words app (https://www.what3words.com) that can assist the emergency services operator identify your location.

Further information regarding calling Triple Zero (000) is available at the following link: https://www.triplezero.gov.au/triple-zero/How-to-Call-000. Use ReachOut or NextStep.

What can I do now? Learn more about signs of an abusive relationship. Talk to someone who understands abusive and violent relationships. Find out more about what to do if you're in an abusive relationship.

You probably know many of the more obvious signs of mental and emotional abuse. But when you're in the midst of it, it can be easy to miss the persistent undercurrent of abusive behavior.

Psychological abuse involves a person's attempts to frighten, control, or isolate you. It's in the abuser's words and actions, as well as their persistence in these behaviors. The abuser can be your spouse or other romantic partner. They could be your business partner, parent, boss, or a caretaker. It doesn't matter who it is, you don't deserve it; and it's not your fault.

Continue reading to learn more, including how to recognize it and what you can do next.

Humiliation, negating, criticizing—these tactics are meant to undermine your self-esteem. The abuse is harsh and unrelenting in matters, big and small.

Here are some examples

Name-calling. They'll blatantly call you "stupid," "a loser," or words too awful to repeat here.

Derogatory "pet names." This is just more name-calling in not-so-subtle disguise. "My little knuckle dragger" or "my chubby pumpkin" aren't terms of endearment.

Character assassination. This usually involves the word "always." You're always late, wrong, screwing up, disagreeable, and so on. Basically, they say you're not a good person.

Yelling, screaming, and swearing. These are meant to intimidate and make you feel small and inconsequential. It might be accompanied by fist pounding or throwing things.

Patronizing. "Aw, sweetie, I know you try, but this is just beyond your understanding."

Public embarrassment. They pick fights, expose your secrets, or make fun of your shortcomings in public.

Dismissiveness. You tell them about something that's important to you, and they say it's nothing.

Body language. Eye-rolling, smirking, headshaking, and sighing help convey the same message.

"Joking." The jokes might have a grain of truth to them or be a complete fabrication. Either way, they make you look foolish.

Sarcasm. This is often just a dig in disguise. When you object, they claim to have been teasing and tell you to stop taking everything so seriously.

Insults of your appearance. They tell you, just before you go out, that your hair is ugly or your outfit is clownish.

Belittling your accomplishments. Your abuser might tell you that your achievements mean nothing, or they may even claim responsibility for your success.

Put-downs of your interests. They might tell you that your hobby is a childish waste of time, or you're out of your league when you play sports. Really, it's that they'd rather you not participate in activities without them.

Pushing your buttons. Once your abuser knows about something that annoys you, they'll bring it up or do it every chance they get.

Control and shame. Trying to make you feel ashamed of your inadequacies is just another path to power.

Monitoring your whereabouts. They want to know where you are all the time and insist that you respond to calls or texts immediately. They might show up just to see if you're where you're supposed to be.

Digital spying. They might check your internet history, emails, texts, and call log. They might even demand your passwords.

Unilateral decision-making. They might close a joint bank account, cancel your doctor's appointment, or speak with your boss without asking.

Financial control. They might keep bank accounts in their name only and make you ask for money. You might be expected to account for every penny you spend.

Lecturing. Belaboring your errors with long monologues, making it clear they think you're beneath them.

Direct orders. From "Get my dinner on the table now" to "Stop taking the pill," orders are expected to be followed despite your plans to the contrary.

Outbursts. You were told to cancel that outing with your friend or put the car in the garage, but you didn't; so now you have to put up with a red-faced tirade about how uncooperative you are.

Treating you like a child. They tell you what to wear, what and how much to eat, or which friends you can see.

Feigned helplessness. They may say they don't know how to do something. Sometimes it's easier to do it yourself than to explain it. They know this and take advantage of it.

Unpredictability. They'll explode with rage out of nowhere, suddenly shower you with affection, or become dark and moody at the drop of a hat to keep you walking on eggshells.

Walking out on you. In a social situation, stomping out of the room leaves you holding the bag. At home, it's a tool to keep the problem unresolved.

Using others. Abusers may tell you that "everybody" thinks you're crazy, or "they all say" you're wrong.

Accusing, blaming, and denial. This behavior comes from an abuser's insecurities. They want to create a hierarchy in which they're at the top, and you're at the bottom. They accuse you of flirting or cheating on them.

Turning the tables. They say you cause their rage and control issues by being such a pain.

Denying something you know is true. An abuser will deny that an argument or even an agreement took place. This is called gaslighting. It's meant to make you question your own memory and sanity.

Using guilt. They might say something like "You owe me this. Look at all I've done for you" in an attempt to get their way.

Goading then blaming. Abusers know just how to upset you. But once the trouble starts, it's your fault for creating it.

Denying their abuse. When you complain about their attacks, abusers will deny it, seemingly bewildered at the very thought of it.

Accusing you of abuse. They say you're the one who has anger and control issues, and they're the helpless victim.

Trivializing. When you want to talk about your hurt feelings, they accuse you of overreacting and making mountains out of molehills.

Saying you have no sense of humor. Abusers make personal jokes about you. If you object, they'll tell you to lighten up.

Blaming you for their problems. Whatever's wrong in their life is all your fault. You're not supportive enough, didn't do enough, or stuck your nose where it didn't belong.

Destroying and denying. They might crack your cell phone screen or "lose" your car keys then deny it.

Emotional neglect and isolation. Abusers tend to place their own emotional needs ahead of yours. Many abusers will try to come between you and people who are supportive of you to make you more dependent on them. They do this by demanding respect. No perceived slight will go unpunished, and you're expected to defer to them. But it's a one-way street.

Shutting down communication. They'll ignore your attempts at conversation in person, by text, or by phone.

Dehumanizing you. They'll look away when you're talking or stare at something else when they speak to you.

Keeping you from socializing. Whenever you have plans to go out, they come up with a distraction or beg you not to go.

Trying to come between you and your family. They'll tell family members that you don't want to see them or make excuses why you can't attend family functions.

Withholding affection. They won't touch you, not even to hold your hand or pat you on the shoulder. They may refuse sexual relations to punish you or to get you to do something.

Tuning you out. They'll wave you off, change the subject, or just plainly ignore you when you want to talk about your relationship.

Actively working to turn others against you. They'll tell coworkers, friends, and even your family that you're unstable and prone to hysterics.

Calling you needy. When you're really down and out and reaching out for support, they'll tell you you're too needy or the world can't stop turning to you for your little problems.

Interrupting. You're on the phone or texting, and they get in your face to let you know your attention should be on them.

Indifference. They see you hurt or crying and do nothing.

Disputing your feelings. Whatever you feel, they'll say you're wrong to feel that way, or that's not really what you feel at all.

Codependency relationship. It is when everything you do is in reaction to your abuser's behavior. And they need you just as much to boost their own self-esteem. You've forgotten how to be any other way. It's a vicious circle of unhealthy behavior.

Signs you might be codependent:

- You are unhappy in the relationship but fear alternatives.
- You consistently neglect your own needs for the sake of theirs.
- You ditch your friends and sideline your family to please your partner.
- You frequently seek out your partner's approval.
- You critique yourself through your abuser's eyes, ignoring your own instincts.
- You make a lot of sacrifices to please the other person, but it's not reciprocated.
- You would rather live in the current state of chaos than be alone.
- You bite your tongue and repress your feelings to keep the peace.

All these are not healthy, and God wants more for you. He didn't put you on earth to take this abuse; so stand your ground and seek help.

What to do

If you're being mentally and emotionally abused, trust your instincts. Know that it isn't right, and you don't have to live this way. If you fear immediate physical violence, call 911 or your local emergency services.

If you aren't in immediate danger and you need to talk or find some place to go, call the National Domestic Abuse hotline at 800-

799-7233. This 24-7 hotline can put you in touch with service providers and shelters across the United States.

Accept that the abuse isn't your responsibility. Don't try to reason with your abuser. You may want to help, but it's unlikely they'll break this pattern of behavior without professional counseling. That's their responsibility. Disengage and set personal boundaries. Decide that you won't respond to abuse or get sucked into arguments. Stick to it. Limit exposure to the abuser as much as you can. Exit the relationship or circumstance. If possible, cut all ties. Make it clear that it's over, and don't look back. You might also want to find a therapist who can show you a healthy way to move forward.

Give yourself time to heal. Reach out to supportive friends and family members. If you're in school, talk to a teacher or guidance counselor. If you think it will help, find a therapist who can help you in your recovery.

Leaving the relationship is more complex if you're married, have children, or have commingled assets. If that's your situation, seek legal assistance. Do not stay in an abusive marriage for the kids' sake. God doesn't want you to live like this, nor does he want your kids to be exposed to this type of behavior. They will grow up affected by it. In the following paragraphs, I'll be talking more about healthy and stable relationships.

To me, there is no real secret to making a relationship work. Communication, trust, honesty, loyalty, respect, caring, and being supportive are just a few ingredients on what it takes to make a relationship last.

Saying I love you to someone is not the same thing as meaning it. Anyone can say I love you, but it all comes down to showing it. Being there for the good and bad times is love. When someone really loves you, they will never give up on being with you, nor will they seek comfort in another person.

When someone tells you this relationship is too much like work, then tell that person to consider yourself fired, or don't bother showing up for work; that is verbal abuse. That is what I have talked about in the previous chapter. Walk away from it because it is not love. I have had that told to me before, and that is why he is an ex.

The person you are with should be talking highly about you. That is love. They should not be talking negatively about you. That is not love.

Let's face it, relationships/marriages take work. It comes down to being a team and giving your whole 100 percent, not 50 percent. There should be 100 percent being shown on both sides.

It is okay to be a little jealous because that just shows how much you love the one you are with, and you are afraid of losing them. But there is a fine line you do not cross, and that is being too overly jealous. That can kill any relationship.

It all comes down to good communication and talking things out, being open with one another. Tell your partner what you are feeling and how you are feeling. Nobody is a mind reader. Don't say everything is fine when it isn't. Don't play mind games either, because all that does is make things worse, and it'll eat you up inside.

The person we are with should be making us feel special, loved, secure, bringing out the best in us, and more. That's the kind of boyfriend I have now. I call him my soulmate because he is someone I've been looking for a long time. I will talk more about him soon.

It is not our job to make anyone happy. Now that would be too much like work. Happiness comes from within. Self-love is so important. People have to find their own happiness. Never look for another to make you happy because you will be alone, waiting and unhappy for a long time. In order to be loved, we must love ourselves first and feel good in our own skin.

When someone is insecure, their insecurity rubs onto us. Therefore, the relationship becomes in jeopardy. Relationships are supposed to blossom like a flower and keep on growing. They are meant to grow into marriage.

You should feel comfortable to be able to talk to your partner about anything and be able to ask questions without them getting mad and feeling threatened. That's what being in a relationship is all about. If you can't do that, then it is not a relationship. It turns out to be a relationship of convenience.

As with anything, time heals all wounds. As time goes on, it does get easier. If there is anything I've learned, it would be that things happen when they are supposed to happen. Just because something isn't happening right now in your life doesn't mean it won't. You just have to be patient and to keep the faith because great things are on the way for you.

Great things happen when we least expect them to. That's how I met my boyfriend, Bobby, of three years. We met on Facebook on February 7, 2018. It was in a group called single to mingle. It is not a dating site. It is a way to make new friends. My friend had added me to this group over a year before he had joined it. I never introduced myself to the group, and then one day I did. It was three days after he had joined that I had introduced myself to the group, but we didn't know that we were both in the group. He saw my post in the group and messaged me, and that was where our love began. As fate and God would have it, I'd say we were meant to be. We clicked from the moment we started chatting on Facebook Messenger. I know we were behind the scenes of the computer from day one, chatting, but we had total chemistry from day one. I would never trade him for another. He has five kids that I get along great with. We've gone on family vacations three times and did some weekend getaways alone. See, I told you great things happen when you least expect them. Stop looking, and love will find you. That is how it happened for us.

I've learned to never give up. You are enough. If your partner can't see how great you are, then he/she isn't for you. The person you are with should be giving you compliments. It doesn't have to be all of the time, but we all love to hear encouraging things and compliments.

Even if you feel good about who you are, it's nice to be told you are handsome/beautiful. I mean, let's face it, as a woman, I love to get told by my boyfriend that I am beautiful, and I look beautiful. He does this by the way. It goes both ways. I give him compliments too.

Breakups aren't easy; but when things don't work out, that just means you are meant to be with another. Never chase after love. If it is not given freely, then move on; otherwise, you'll just end up hurting yourself in the end. Keep this in mind, when you are hurting, you are the only one hurting. The other person is going to go on with their business and life. Life isn't long enough to be anything but happy. We all deserve to be with someone who makes us feel good. Never settle. Let love find you. It found me.

The chapter may have been called "When Your Heart Breaks—Mental/Physical Abuse," but it has a happy ending to it, don't you think?

Chapter 4

LEARNING TO LET GO

It is not always easy when it comes to letting go. I'm not just talking about relationships; I'm talking about learning to let go of things like friendships that aren't healthy. Friendships that don't bring us happiness but bring toxicity to our lives need to be set free. I know it is not always an easy decision to make; but if we want our life to blossom like God wants it to blossom, then it won't happen if we have these types of friends. I mention this a lot; but remember that life, as we know, is not long enough for friends that are not going to bring out the best of you. God will remove these kinds of friends and have great friends enter our lives. This scripture really jumps out at me: "My Christian friends, remember to be happy even when many kinds of trouble happen to you" (James 1:2). Troubles can help you. This is so true because being in troubled times will make us stronger.

Friendships are a two-way street. They are based on honesty, trust, communication, and so much more. Living life without drama and negativity is the way to live. You can't have a house without first having the foundation, so why would you want friends who are not going to be real with you?

Back in the day, I thought I had friends whom I could trust, only to find out, I could not. I like to give people the benefit of the doubt. I trust easily, and I like to see the good in people. Nowadays though, I feel people out, and I go with my gut. I will still be nice to people, but I will not be so trusting. I have to say though, I feel blessed for the friends I do have in my life. For the people whom we thought were our friends, all we can do is pray over them and wish them well in life. Revenge and being bitter is a waste of time. In order to live an abundant life that God has given us, we need to learn to leave them in the past and move forward.

It is unfortunate, and I dislike to say this, but there are people in this world who are jealous, don't like to see when we are happy, will do anything to make sure others are miserable, and anything else that doesn't stem from positiveness. Some people would rather see others miserable because they are not happy with themselves and with their own life. Like I said, I know this sounds harsh, but as we go through living our life's journey, we find it to be true. Now I'm not saying everyone is like this; I most certainly am not. But we can't go through life with blinders on, thinking everyone is for us.

You see, God did not make people to be this way. He made us full of life and to love one another. He designed our life to be more than average. He does not want us to live feeling stuck in life. He wants us to grow, learn, and do more with the life he has given us. He wants us to live an abundant life; walk in faith, not by sight; find love, not hate; live positively; and so much more.

When I pray, I ask God to put me on the path of life that he has meant for me to be on. Sometimes we take the wrong path in life; but when we turn our lives over to Jesus and seek him for guidance, then that is when our lives change for the better. I know this to be true because I have done this myself. My life has changed for the better because I gave my life over to Jesus. Like I said, it is not easy to let go of the old life we were once living. It is not going to happen overnight; but taking the first step is a big move in the right direction. Amen.

I love seeing others do great in life. I love seeing people succeed. Do you know why? It's because God loves this too. It puts a blessing on my heart to see others do great in life. This is one of many reasons why I wrote this book. I live to inspire. It makes me feel good when I'm helping others. I love to give encouragement as well. God is always helping me do this as well.

When we are in an unhealthy relationship, it is toxic to our health. Sometimes we don't even know we are in one. Outsiders can see that it is toxic. But because we are in the relationship, it is hard to see it. Sometimes some of us can see it is a toxic relationship, but it is hard to let go, maybe because we are afraid of being alone, or we are afraid to escape it if our partner is threatening us.

Sometimes people have a way of manipulating us by making us feel guilty for everything. They force their insecurities on us. They make us doubt ourselves. They also make us responsible for their emotions. They make us believe that we want the same thing that they want. It is unhealthy being in a relationship with someone like this, let alone being around people who are like this. It is hard to know at first when we get involved with someone that they are like this. That's why it is important to not ignore the red flags. It is not easy to do because we want to see the good in people. We don't want to believe and see the truth. If and when you are in doubt, write it in a journal and pray to God about it; and he will lead you to the truth. I'm very happy to say that with my boyfriend, there has never been any red flags. In the next paragraphs, I'm going to give you some red flags of a narcissist.

They feel like they have a sense of entitlement. Everyone deserves things like equal protection under the law; but narcissists think they are particularly entitled. If they don't get their own way, they become upset because in a narcissist's mind, the world is supposed to revolve around them. Moments in life are positive because they are entitled to them. Negative moments aren't supposed to happen to them. The world, as we know it, is not going to be fair for everyone; but narcissists can believe this is a personal slight against them and not just a matter of bad luck or unfortunate circumstances. When one can't begin to understand the concept of rolling with the punches, they are likely a narcissist.

Some signs of a narcissist are the following:

Narcissists have short-term relationships. They are so focused on themselves and their egos that cause them not to be in relationships for very long. These individuals often look for someone who can make them satisfied with their sense of self-worth, which would be seen as infidelity in many cases. In other words, they want a friend that would take care of their demands and meet their needs. Without mutual benefits and communication, it is easy to understand why these relationships often end soon. Their partners or friends are often unsatisfactory to these narcissists and might break up once they realize the problems.

Some people that are narcissists do not even realize they are.

Narcissists often place higher values on their outward appearances than other people. These people use their looks as a way to promote their current status and achieve their desires. Thus, they tend to spend plenty of time choosing clothing or styling their hair. Their clothing is usually expensive and flashy. Women with narcissism also tend to show off their cleavage and wear makeup. While this is not always an obvious sign as each person might have different tastes about fashion and appearance, many narcissists would draw you in immediately due to the way they are attempting to make a good impression.

Narcissists always believe that they are the most competent, the most skilled, and the best person in a team or a group. This can be seen clearly in how they do everything in their own way. In addition, these people might want to control everyone and own everything.

Another possible sign of narcissism is perfectionism. People with this condition always have an extreme need for everything to be perfect. From events and jobs to family and pets, they always believe that these things should meet their expectations and happen precisely as expected.

You can look for self-references in narcissists. This means that they often keep the discussion to themselves. It does not matter how relevant or suitable it is to the theme; people with this condition tend to find an anecdote or story which can place them in the center of the conversation.

There are many other ways people may be a narcissist too: lack of empathy, they tend to focus on themselves and strive for attention, and they always need constant attention from others.

As with many personality disorders, the exact cause of narcissistic personality disorder (NPD) is unknown. It is probably a mixture of genes, early childhood experiences, and psychological factors.

Early childhood risk factors include insensitive parenting, over-praising, and excessive pampering (when parents focus intensely on a particular talent or the physical appearance of their child as a result of their own self-esteem issues)

Unpredictable or negligent care:

- excessive criticism
- abuse
- trauma
- extremely high expectations
- being oversensitive

Other possible factors include abnormalities in the genes that affect the connection between the brain and behavior. Although there is no one answer to the question of what causes NPD, professionals agree that the sooner treatment begins, the better a person's chance for an improved quality of life.

There is a positive side to all of this kind of behavior. If you know someone who is like this, you can help them by having them seek counseling for it. If they are aware of how they are acting and behaving, then they have to be willing to want to change their behavior.

As I have stated before, some people are unaware that they even are behaving this way. There's no cure for narcissistic personality disorder (NPD), but talking to a professional can help. The foundation of NPD treatment will be psychotherapy. This is often a mixture of individual, group, and family therapies to help an individual understand the causes of their beliefs, behavior, and learn ways of relating to others. The goal is to build up the person's poor self-esteem and have more realistic expectations of others.

Narcissists can learn how to relate to others in more positive ways, but it depends on how open they are to critical feedback and how willing they are to change. If they don't want to change their ways, then you must move on. Break free from this type of behavior so you can abundantly live the life God gave you. Continue to pray for them and for them to seek God so they can live their life abundantly as well.

I was once married. We got married on October 27, 2005. It didn't work out. It was one of the hardest decisions I had to make for myself. I was thirty years old when I got married. I waited to have sex until I was married. I wanted it to be with someone I was going to be with forever. But unfortunately, things do not always turn out like we planned them to. I've dated a few guys before I got married, but they were not worth dating for very long, for they were only out for one thing. Now I just look at it like I was not meant to be with them. At the time, I felt hurt; and it took a while to let go. Even though my marriage did not work out, I'm happy that I waited to have sex until I was married. I will get into why it was a hard decision to get divorced soon.

When people do not understand why we do the things we do, they tend to paint their own picture on how they want to see things. Or let's just say, that's how they want to see it because it makes them feel better about themselves. If people are not happy with themselves, then that's what they will do. We may get judged as well. One thing to keep in mind is to not listen to what others are saying and thinking. They are not walking in our shoes, nor are they living the same life as we are. Until people have walked in another's shoes, then they really don't know what the other person has gone through or is going through. I never ever judge another soul because I do not want to be judged, and I don't know what that other person is going through or has gone through. I always say, treat others like you want to be treated. It all comes down to the golden rule.

We owe nobody any explanation as to why we do what we do.

Before my ex-husband and I got married, we had dated for two years. Eight months after we had dated, he got tested for Huntington's disease. His sister was noticing some symptoms in him that were related to the disease. His mom had it. You can only get it from a parent who has it. Some people can be carriers where they will never get the symptoms; they'll just be carriers—meaning, they can pass

44

it onto their children. When his mom had kids, she never knew she had it. She found out she had HD in her forties. My ex-husband got tested when he found out his mom had it. At the time, he was in the army. They did the test, and it came back negative. I'm not sure what type of test they did. So he thought he was in the clear.

He has two other sisters. One of his sisters doesn't have it. At the time, his other sister did not want to get tested, so I don't know if she has it or not.

My ex-husband Ted's sister went with him to get tested for Huntington's disease. They went to Uconn in Farmington, Connecticut. This was back in August of 2003. They did a blood test there. When the results came back weeks later, I was heartbroken. I did not want it to be positive, but he tested positive for HD. We were in love, so I stayed with him and married him, knowing he had this awful disease. I'll tell you more about what Huntington's disease is soon.

I thought we would have many years together because of it being a slow-moving disease. The slow-moving doctors were talking about how he wouldn't wake up in a wheelchair the next day. His sister tried telling me that it was a big responsibility. But like with everything, we do not always know what to expect until we are in the situation.

We were married for four years. It came to a point where I could not take care of him anymore. I was thirty-four when we got divorced. He went to live with his stepmom and her husband but not for very long. She had to put him in a home in Rocky Hill where he could get better care. It was a home for veterans. Since he was a veteran, he was able to go live there.

Like I said, it was a hard decision to make. I felt guilty because I married him, and now we were getting divorced. I did not leave him because of his disease. Obviously, I married him knowing he had HD. People would judge me, saying how could I leave my sick husband, which was not the case. It goes back to what I was saying before. Nobody should judge anybody especially if they haven't been in that person's shoes. I was still young and had to work to survive.

I would never wish this disease on anyone. It is awful and crippling. It changes the person's overall well-being. It is sad and heartbreaking to have to see someone go through this. I was mad, bitter, and angry that all this was happening. How could this happen to someone who was so kind, sweet, caring, fought for our country, and more? Life is definitely not fair at times. It has been twelve years since we've been divorced, and it is still hard, knowing that the rest of his life won't be easy sailing. I pray that God heals and protects him.

I feel that if I had God in my life back in the day, I would have heard his voice, and I would have asked him for more of a direction on what I should have done. I would have asked if I should marry Ted. I have a feeling the answer would have been no because looking back, God would have known it would be a short-lived marriage. I'm not saying I didn't believe in God back then; but what I'm saying is if I would have let God into my life more then, I believe things would have been different.

In the next paragraphs, I'll go into a little of what Huntington's disease is.

It is a neurological disease that affects the muscles, motor skills, the functioning of the brain, and more. Huntington's disease is a rare, inherited disease that causes the progressive breakdown (degeneration) of nerve cells in the brain. Huntington's disease has a broad impact on a person's functional abilities and usually results in movement, thinking (cognitive), and psychiatric disorders. Huntington's disease symptoms can develop at any time, but they often first appear when people are in their thirties or forties. If the condition develops before age twenty, it's called juvenile Huntington's disease. When Huntington's develops early, the symptoms are somewhat different, and the disease may progress faster. Medications are available to help manage the symptoms of Huntington's disease; but treatments can't prevent the physical, mental, and behavioral decline associated with the condition.

Symptoms of Huntington's disease usually cause movement, cognitive, and psychiatric disorders with a wide spectrum of signs and symptoms. Which symptoms appear first vary greatly from person to person. Some symptoms appear more dominant or have a greater effect on functional ability, but that can change throughout the course of the disease.

The movement disorders associated with Huntington's disease can include both involuntary movement problems and impairments in voluntary movements, such as the following:

- Involuntary jerking or writhing movements (chorea)
- Muscle problems, such as rigidity or muscle contracture (dystonia)
- Slow or abnormal eye movements
- Impaired gait, posture, and balance
- Difficulty with speech or swallowing
- Impairments in voluntary movements rather than the involuntary movements—may have a greater impact on a person's ability to work, perform daily activities, communicate, and remain independent

Cognitive impairments often associated with Huntington's disease include the following:

- Difficulty organizing, prioritizing, or focusing on tasks
- Lack of flexibility or the tendency to get stuck on a thought, behavior, or action (perseveration)
- Lack of impulse control that can result in outbursts, acting without thinking, and sexual promiscuity
- Lack of awareness of one's own behaviors and abilities
- Slowness in processing thoughts or "finding" words
- Difficulty in learning new information

The most common psychiatric disorder associated with Huntington's disease is depression. This isn't simply a reaction to receiving a diagnosis of Huntington's disease, instead, depression appears to occur because of injury to the brain and subsequent changes in brain function. Signs and symptoms may include the following:

- Feelings of irritability, sadness, or apathy
- Social withdrawal

- Insomnia
- Fatigue and loss of energy
- Frequent thoughts of death, dying, or suicide
- Other common psychiatric disorders include the following:
- Obsessive-compulsive disorder, a condition marked by recurrent, intrusive thoughts, and repetitive behaviors
- Mania, which can cause elevated mood, overactivity, impulsive behavior, and inflated self-esteem
- Bipolar disorder, a condition with alternating episodes of depression and mania

In addition to the above disorders, weight loss is common in people with Huntington's disease, especially as the disease progresses.

Symptoms of juvenile Huntington's disease: The start and progression of Huntington's disease in younger people may be slightly different from that in adults.

Problems that often present early in the course of the disease include the following:

- Behavioral changes
- Difficulty paying attention
- Rapid, significant drop in overall school performance
- Behavioral problems
- Physical changes
- Contracted and rigid muscles that affect gait (especially in young children)
- Tremors or slight involuntary movement
- Frequent falls or clumsiness
- Seizures

Huntington's disease is caused by an inherited defect in a single gene. Huntington's disease is an autosomal dominant disorder, which means that a person needs only one copy of the defective gene to develop the disorder. With the exception of genes on the sex chromosomes, a person inherits two copies of every gene—one copy from each parent. A parent with a defective gene can pass along the defective copy of the gene or the healthy copy. Each child in the family, therefore, has a 50 percent chance of inheriting the gene that causes the genetic disorder.

After Huntington's disease starts, a person's functional abilities gradually worsen over time. The rate of disease progression and duration varies. The time from disease emergence to death is often about ten to thirty years. Juvenile Huntington's disease usually results in death within ten years after symptoms develop.

The clinical depression associated with Huntington's disease may increase the risk of suicide. Some research suggests that the greater risk of suicide occurs before a diagnosis is made and in the middle stages of the disease when a person starts to lose independence. Eventually, a person with Huntington's disease requires help with all activities of daily living and care. Late in the disease, he or she will likely be confined to a bed and unable to speak. Someone with Huntington's disease is generally able to understand language and has an awareness of family and friends, though some won't recognize family members.

Common causes of death include the following:

- Pneumonia or other infection
- Injuries related to falls
- Complications related to the inability to swallow
- Prevention

As you can see how hard this was on me—and it was hard letting go—in my heart, I felt it was a good decision. I felt guilty for the longest time. Here I was, able to go on and live a normal life, and here was Ted who was not able to do the same. It was hard to have to go through, but God got me through.

My ex-boyfriend of five years, Ed, that I have mentioned in the beginning of the book would judge me for this and use it against me. He would talk behind my back and tell people that I left my sick husband. I was so hurt by this. I was like, how dare he? He had no right to say that since he was not the one who had to go through what I went through.

Today, I do not have bitterness over it. I've learned to let it go, forgive, and pray for him. It is not worth dwelling over. It is not worth holding on to things that do not matter. All it does is bring us down, and the enemy wins. God forgave me and forgave us; so with that, we shall forgive too. God died for our sins; so with that, God forgives us all.

There is this scripture that I love, and it speaks volumes. It is this: Do not become angry with each other. If you think that someone has done something wrong against you, forgive them. Remember that the Lord has forgiven you (Colossians 3:13). So you should also forgive other people. This is something I definitely live by. Today, I do not care what people say about me because they are not God. God knows what is going to happen before we know it. That's why it's so important to seek him and ask him what we should do before we do it. When Jesus says something, pay attention. If he says it three times, change your perspective. Today I pray more, and I ask God to lead me on the right journey in life that he has designed for me.

My boyfriend knows about my past, and he does not judge me. I do not judge him either. We treat one another with respect and so much more. Now that is love, and that's one of many reasons why I love him and why I am with him. When we meet our soul mate, we realize this is how we are supposed to be treated. Letting go from the one we were with before makes us realize they were not the one we were meant to be with. Being in the relationship, we don't see it until we are away from the situation we were once in.

Relationships aren't that hard. Yeah, they take work; but what doesn't? As long as you have many good days and not many stress days together, then that is all that matters. I'm not talking about the stresses in life because that is something that we can't control. When two people have a connection, trust each other, love one another, are open and honest, have no lies nor secrets, it is magical. This is how relationships/marriages are all about.

Chapter 5

LIVING A
BITTERLESS LIFE

When someone does us wrong, it is easy to want to seek revenge. We want them to suffer. We seek anger and hatred when we should be seeking Jesus. I know it is not easy to just let it go and move on, but it is not a way to live. If we want a better life, then we have to change our ways. Let God take care of the ones who do us wrong. Be a better person, and don't seek revenge. Instead, just move on and wish that person well. This is a great scripture: Do not get angry quickly. That is what fools do (Ecclesiastes 7:9). Try to forget the bad things that people may have done to you. This is what I do too. I believe that taking revenge is not worth it. The best thing we can do for ourselves is walk away and don't look back. Amen.

In order to have a better day is to remain strong and be a better person. Choose to not let things get the best of you. Choose to smile more and not get angry when someone cuts you off in the line at the grocery store or when you are driving. When someone gives you a hard time at work, home, the store, and anywhere else, keep calm and carry on. Breathe in and out. And if it is possible, regroup. Here's a scripture that will help: Do not become angry or upset. It will only bring trouble for you (Psalm 37:8).

I understand the whole thing of not letting people get the best of us. I'm a hairstylist, so I get it. Some clients are not the easiest to satisfy. Don't get me wrong, I love what I do; but there are some days that I want to pull my own hair out. Okay, so I'm exaggerating. There will be moments when kids' moms and dads hover over me when I try to cut their child's hair, and I want to just tell them to sit down. I mean, I don't; but I admit, it drives me crazy. My anxiety level goes up; so because of that, I might come off as being stand-offish. When clients do this, it makes me feel like I don't know what I'm doing. When they leave the salon, I regroup. This way, I'm not uptight when I take the next client.

I'm telling you this because we are human, and things like this will happen. I realized it is not worth letting it get the best of me since they are not in the salon very long. I've gotten a lot better with not letting my emotions and anxiety get the best of me though.

The devil loves to see us get anxious, mad, annoyed, frustrated, and everything that doesn't stem from the positive fruit. When this happens, I say, "Blood of Jesus" or "Holy Spirit" because the enemy fears it and backs off. Jesus rules and wants us to be happy. I love when I win the fight over the enemy. I love God and for all he has done in my life too. When this happens to you, try it because it does help.

Living a bitterless life is also about letting go of jealous behavior. Life is too beautiful to be jealous of another soul. Be happy with yourself and with what God has given you. If we look at what others have and what we don't, it'll just cause us to act jealous and be ungrateful for what we do have.

I'm not a jealous person at all. I don't own my own house. I have friends who own their own homes; but I don't care because I'm happy and content with what I do have. I am very happy for them, and that is how it should be.

We all want what the other has. We want to be better than the other person. We get discouraged when others do better than us. This type of behavior won't make your life great. Instead, it will make you more bitter and jealous.

The way you can overcome this is to just focus on you and nobody else. Focus on what you have and your achievements. Look in the mirror, and love what you see. If you are not happy with what you see, you are going to always be miserable, jealous, and bitter. You must look deep inside your soul to find happiness with yourself.

If you can't stand yourself, then that's going to be a problem because you are around yourself more than you are around others. We have to be our own inspirations and cheerleaders. It's good to hear compliments from others; but don't expect to get them. If you do, then you will continue to get discouraged. Self-love is so important.

I'm not bitter and jealous because I choose not to be this way. We have to want to live life like this. There is no hidden secret. In order to change our ways, we gotta want to do it. Nobody can do it for us. Well honestly, God can help us, but he can only help us if we allow him to. He gives us free will to make our own decisions. In the following paragraphs, I will help you overcome being jealous, bitter, and more.

Find a quiet place to spend time alone. This is very important to do now and then. You cannot be lonely if you like the person you are alone with. If you love who you are and are at peace with who you are, then you won't mind being alone. When you are alone, don't be on your phone. Shut it off so you can have total alone time by yourself without getting interrupted.

Allow yourself to feel your emotion, but this does not mean indiging in it. We become jealous because we think our friends have a perfect life and feel our life isn't great. Well let me tell you, nobody has a perfect life because nothing is perfect. Everyone has problems. The only difference is some people have bigger problems than the other person has.

Explore what important lesson the emotion is trying to teach you. Remember that other people mirror how we feel about ourselves. The negative fruit of jealousy and bitterness are fear and sadness. So if people make you jealous and bitter, you are only really fearful and pessimistic about your own sense of self-worth.

You might ask, "How can the feeling of jealousy change in my life?" The answer is any negative thing in your life can be changed into something positive if you let it. For example, when we let jealousy in our lives, it teaches us how to improve both internally as a person and in our eternal life. Other emotions, like resentment toward other people, may teach you about your tendency to hold grudges against others and how you are your own harshest critic.

Another way you can let go of bitterness and jealousy is realizing that you are this way. Some of us are unaware we are this way. If you are feeling resentment and hatred, then you tend to act out. You tend to be negative. This is no way to live. And the best thing you can do for yourself is let go and move forward.

You may think that your workplace is toxic; but is it the workplace that is toxic or your thoughts about it? A concrete jungle is a concrete jungle. It is neither a "good" or "bad" place. Rather, it is your mental perceptions that judge if it is good or bad and consequently. It is your thoughts that create your misery. You can approach your life situation as an opportunity to grow or to be defeated. And besides, what lasts forever? If you can change your circumstances, do so; but be aware that a fault-finding mindset will always be unhappy wherever it goes. If you can't change your circumstance, repeat the previous points that I've discussed and learn to reframe your perspective. You can either be the victim of your reality or the hero of it.

Take time out from your friendships or relationships. Give yourself space to breathe. If you fear that you are on the verge of destroying something precious, let your friend or partner know that you need time alone to unwind and relax. This way, you will create a temporary buffer that will allow you to explore how you feel and what to do about it. You can also write in a journal of why you are feeling the way you are feeling. Write down why you were/are jealous and bitter of a given situation. Take all this good, healthy information, and fill your soul with it. Refer back to these paragraphs; and if it helps, write them in your journal as well.

You see, when we are bitter, jealous, angry, mad, and everything else that does not stem from good, we not only affect ourselves, but we affect others around us. Our attitude rubs onto others and causes that person to be in a bad mood. God designed us to be more like him so we can make more disciples. By being this way, we are not setting good examples for others. Therefore, we can't do the work God designed us to do.

Life, as we know, is precious. We don't know what is going to happen from one minute to the next, so why waste it on being bitter, negative, mad, jealous, and more? Put your precious time into motion on positive things, like working on yourself, your self-esteem, and being happy with who you are and all you have. Amen.

People will say things and talk negatively behind our backs. The best thing we can do for ourselves is ignore it. What they're saying about us is none of our business, nor should we let it consume us. Trust me, I've learned this the hard way. I would let it consume me, until one day I said, "I am not going to let it take up space in my head." If it did, I was going to have to charge it for rent.

I used to live life bitterly too; and then one day, I decided it was not worth it. I decided to change my ways. I realized that life is not long enough to live it this way. This is one of the many reasons of how I came to write my book. I wanted to be able to help others to not live this way, that it's not healthy, nor is it wise.

As we grow, we mature and realize what matters most, like family and good friends. We are given choices, either we let go of bitterness or we keep letting it dormant in our souls. In the end, we are the ones hurting if we don't let go of it.

People will say things behind our backs and not be real. That's just the way it is. Not everyone is going to be for us, and that's okay. It's up to us to not have this affect us. We have control on how we will handle things. We have control on how we will respond to things.

What I do every morning when I wake up is pray. As I pray, there are a few things that I keep in mind to pray for. I ask God to help me make all the right decisions for my upcoming day and for him to help me to respond to people in a positive way even when they are not being so nice.

God gives us free will to do things; but when we seek him and ask him what we should do, we are sparing ourselves from pain, discouragement, disappointment, aggravation, and more.

What I do is spread love in the world because there is too much unkindness and bitterness in the world. I smile and say hello to strangers, I open doors for others, and treat others like I want to be treated. All these make me feel good. Instead of hating people, I choose not to. I throw kindness like confetti.

Everyone deserves to be happy. Life, as we know, isn't long enough to be anything but happy. For the ones who are not for me or dislike me, I still want nothing but happiness for them.

Another reason why I wrote this book is for others to be loved, feel loved, be inspired, spread positive energy, know God is always there whenever we seek him, and so much more.

When something is bothering you, when someone is being difficult, upsetting you, take a couple of deep breaths, count to ten, exhale, and regroup. Do not act on this type of behavior. Ignore it. Tell yourself that you aren't going to let this get the best of you. When you do this, you'll be happy you did.

I'm not saying it's easy to control getting mad, frustrated, irritated, and more. I myself know it isn't easy. Heck, I do it. We all do it. We are human. It is going to happen from time to time. We just have to learn how to manage it from happening all of the time. It's when we let it linger on that it becomes a problem. Don't let it linger on throughout your day and into the next day. I was once like this. I would let things pry on my mind. I would overanalyze. I overcame it by regrouping and by being alone. Things become clearer when we take time to be by ourselves.

I wasn't always the same person I am today. I mean, I've always been loving, caring, loyal, honest, sweet, kind, considerate, and so forth. I am still that person. That has not changed. I've just grown more comfortable in my skin. What I mean by that is I'm more positive, not bitter, and I've gotten control over my life by not letting people or things get the best of me. God has a lot to do with that. I pray and get answers. I'm happy with the person I have become, and you can also become happy with the person you've become too.

Life, as we know, isn't long enough. You will see me mention that quite often as I have already. I tend to repeat so it will help sink in. Life is not long enough to live in the past. We just have to learn to let things go and move on. Nobody can make this choice for us. We have to want to do it. Nobody can tell us not to be bitter. We have that choice not to be. I can't, and I will never tell someone what to do. I can only give the best advice that I can give. If we want to change, we have to let go of our old ways and live for today and not tomorrow. Living a bitterless life is a work in progress, but I have faith you will overcome it. Amen.

Chapter 6

DARE TO BE UNIQUE

Too many times, we want to be like everyone else. We want what the other person has. For example, if they have highlights in their hair, then we want it too. If others have short hair, we want that style too. Same goes for long hair.

As a hairstylist, I will get clients in my chair, and they'll ask me what the latest hairstyle is. My response is there is no style. The style is whatever you like. I mean, I will give suggestions, but I want them to have a haircut or style that is suitable for their face and their own uniqueness. They are happy with my approach and my suggestions.

I love being a hairstylist. I love interacting with people. I love helping people feel their best. These and more are many reasons why I became a hairstylist. It has been ten years since I've been a hairstylist, and I am happy with my career choice.

Other examples of how we want to be like others is if someone has a nice car, house, shoes, clothes, and more, we want to buy these things too. If they just bought a car, house, or anything else, we want to buy the same thing. If someone is going to college, we want to go too. If someone is getting married, we also want to get married. By now, I think you know where I am going with all of this. This, my friends, is not going to bring you happiness or keep you unique. In fact, it is just going to bring you misery, unhappiness, etc. It is not going to come from anything good because you are trying to keep up with what your friends and family have. You are being too focused on what the other person has and does not have instead of focusing on yourself. It is not a healthy way to live. To be honest, I do not do this because I am satisfied with what I have.

In a bit, I will help you overcome this too.

Some people want to be like others instead of being themselves. They think, *Well if I have the same style in clothes, then I will fit in with the crowd.* That's not the case. Because if people like you, then that won't matter. They will want to be around you for your uniqueness, kindness, and more. Good friends are not going to like you for what you have; they are going to like you regardless of what you have. If they don't, then they were never your friends from the beginning.

We tend to want the lives of others because we think their lives are better than our own. Truth be told, their lives aren't any better than ours. We must stop comparing and just be happy with what we have. Like I said before, in order to succeed in life and get what we want out of life, we must run our own race and stop comparing ourselves to one another. We need to look ahead and not worry about what the other person is doing. We all walk different paths in life. If we continue to compare, then we will never get ahead in life.

Be unique, and be like no other. After all, we are different from one another. I mean, if we were all alike, how boring would that be? I love being unique and not having what others have.

So I've told you how being unique is great. Now I am going to help you on how you can be unique, grateful for what you have, and more in the next paragraphs.

One way you can achieve being unique is by reflecting on your good qualities. Examples of good qualities can be things like kindness, being loving, being caring, honesty, truth, having compassion for others, being considerate, etc.

Write down on a piece of paper or in a journal what sets you apart from others. This could be something you're great at, like sports, singing, dancing, writing, swimming, cooking, cleaning, etc. Write down what you love about yourself. This could be your eyes, hair, body, personality, attitude, and more. Brisk walking or running can help give you clarity.

Other examples of wanting to be unique and grateful for what you have is to write it down in a journal. This will help you not want what others have. It will also help you appreciate what you do have.

More examples of these having a roof over your head, clothing, job, friends, family, marriage, relationship, happiness, health, and more.

Other examples of being unique can be being silly, funny, doing things to make you happy, being a rebel, being daring, taking risks, succeeding in your goals, believing in yourself, not caring about what people think of you and say about you, and more.

One of the many ways that I am unique is that I don't care what others think of me. I don't care what people are saying about me. I am silly most of the time. I act crazy and happy—well in a good way, that is. People may look at me like I am weird, but I don't care. I speak the truth. I tell it like it is—well in a nice way. I am not a quick learner, but that's fine. When I catch on to doing something, I never forget how to do it. I am not the fastest person when it comes to doing things, and that's fine too. I don't think I am the best hairstylist around, but I do not compete to be the best. I will tell you who I do to compete with, and that is me. I compete to be the best version of myself every day. I run my own race. I'm happy how far I've come in my career. I don't look to impress others. I am me, and I will never change. Nobody should ever change to make another happy. This is what being unique is all about. If people can't accept you for your unique qualities, then they don't deserve to be around you.

You need to surround yourself with people who are going to bring out the best in you, not people who are going to tear you down. So you talk fast, your speech isn't that great, you are a little overweight, you may be short or too tall, you don't catch on to things that quickly, and so forth. Who cares? You might say this, "But I am not perfect." Well guess what? Nobody is. Be who you are, be okay with it, and be like nobody else.

So you don't wear what's in style. Who cares? There is no style. We have our own style. That's what being unique means as well. To be honest, I never understood why people care what is in style or why others feel like they have to dress like others. I say, be your own kind of style.

When you are feeling uncertain about yourself, think about all the positive traits you have. Think about all the things you have accomplished and more things you will accomplish. Think about how great of a person you are and a blessing you are to others. This will help you feel great about who you are. It will also strengthen your weaknesses.

Here's a great scripture that touches my heart.

> And now these three remain: faith, hope, and love. But the greatest of these is love. (1 Corinthians 3:13)

This is something I always say: In order to be loved, we must learn to love ourselves first.

Being unique is an awesome way to be. I used to think that there was something wrong with me because it would take me longer to learn things than anyone else. I would be like, "Why can't I learn quickly like everyone else can?" For instance, when I was in a hairdressing school, students would catch on quickly on how to cut hair, highlights, perms, etc. on the mannequins; but then there was me who couldn't grasp it right away. That made me frustrated and annoyed. Today I realize that there is nothing wrong with me. It just means I catch on at a different pace, and it makes me unique from everyone else, which is fine because I love being different. Having a learning disability, taking longer to learn something, etc. doesn't mean you are stupid; so never ever feel you are. It's called having a unique trait.

May all this help you and give you clarity on how to be unique and how to live life with a grateful heart.

It never hurts to reread things. It actually helps us to remember things better and for it to sink in our brains. As a matter of fact, I sometimes have to read things a few times before something makes sense to me. Heck, never mind that. As I am typing up my book, I have to read it a few times to make sure it makes sense. That's another one of my unique traits.

Chapter 7

LOVE AGAIN

It is hard to trust again when we've gotten our hearts broken so many times. We feel like we will never find that person we are meant to be with. We may feel like everyone is the same. We may keep our walls up to prevent us from getting hurt again. We may even want to hurt others because we've been hurt by others.

Well that is not a good approach to take because not everyone is our ex. We can't hurt others just because others have hurt us, nor should we take it out on another person. When we hurt others, there are consequences for our actions. God sees what is going on. He does not like this behavior.

If we want to be better people, then we have to start off by treating others how we want to be treated. I say, God calls us to be disciples and for us to make more disciples like himself.

When we stop looking for love and for that person God has chosen for us to be with, that's when God will send that person into our lives. Just because you haven't found love yet doesn't mean it will never happen for you.

The one thing we cannot do is to bring up past relationships into the other one, otherwise it is not going to work. I've done this, and it just causes more harm than good. We can't compare our current relationship with our old one. If we do this, then we will never find love.

When relationships don't work out, it just means we are meant to be with someone else. We don't always see this at the time because we are in the relationship. But give it a few weeks or even a few months, and you will see that you are meant to be with another.

Like I said before, we can't bring up our past relationships into the current one nor should we do the comparison because we don't live there anymore. What I mean by that is we are in a better place in our life, and we are no longer living in that life anymore.

In the Scripture, Psalm 37:5 says, "Let the Lord be your guide into the future. Trust in him and he will help you." If you are ever in doubt about the relationship you are in, refer back to this scripture, and the Lord will lead you in the right direction This goes with anything in life as well. Pray for God to help lead you on the right path in life too.

I never understood why people play games. I am always like, "Why can't people just be honest and tell the person they don't want to be in a relationship?" Some will be up-front with you, but those are the ones who are not players. The ones who are players will not be up-front with you. They might even make you think they want a relationship; but in reality, they don't. In the next paragraph, I will get into more of this.

When people are hurting, they tend to play mind games. Because some people have been hurt in the past, they may end up also turning into players and such. Sometimes, people don't even have to get hurt to be players. It is just in them to be this way. Some just like the thrill of it. They like the challenge, or they just aren't feeling good about themselves. They are insecure with themselves and more, so they play games.

We must watch the signs of this. People who tend to do this are the ones who won't commit. They will hide you from the world. They will just want to hook up. When you try to make plans with them, they will make an excuse to not want to meet up. But when they hit you up in the spur of the moment, and it is unplanned chances, they are looking for a booty call. Look for the signs, and be mindful of this behavior. It is sad why people do this; and it is wrong. But don't get caught up in it. Instead, walk away, and don't look back.

I know all this to be true because I met a few men like this, but God helped me to see the signs. I did not give them what they wanted. Instead, I walked away. God has a better plan for you and does not want you to be caught up in this behavior either. Remember this too, when someone is into you, they are not going to want to take you to bed on the first date. They will want to get to know you better.

I get it. Learning how to love and trust again is not easy. They say you'll know when the right one comes along. I believe this to be true to some degree. I believe you have to get to know someone really well before jumping to that conclusion. Once you get to know the person well enough, that is when you will know that they are the right person for you. We tend to know if it is going to work after a few months or sooner of being with someone.

It is awesome if there is chemistry, but that is not all there is to making a relationship last. You have to have things in common with that person. Trust, honesty, understanding, communication, loyalty, laughter, etc. play an important part in any relationship. If you don't have this then move on. Life, as we know, isn't long enough to settle.

The best advice I can give anyone when it comes to relationships is to take it slow. Rushing into something tends to end before it even blossoms into something. Let things happen naturally and on their own. Take things as they come. Forcing something to happen won't work. It will just cause misery.

Unfortunately, some people can fool us into thinking they are someone who they are not. If you have doubts, questions, and see the red flags, get out of the relationship. Don't even try to make it work or reason with it. It is not worth overanalyzing and questioning it.

When we are looking for someone to make us happy, it isn't going to work. If we do this, then we will never be happy. We must learn to be happy on our own. We cannot depend on others to fulfill our happiness and the emptiness that we feel inside our souls.

Do things that will make you happy, like shopping, helping others out, singing, dancing, drawing, etc.; but first, be happy with yourself.

If there is anything I've learned, it would be to give yourself time to heal before getting involved with another. Give yourself a chance to get to know yourself and to figure out what it is you want in a relationship. When we do this, it will give you clarity. Get together with friends and have fun. Go away for a weekend. Go on that vacation you have been putting on hold. Take some time for yourself, and just be you.

A lot of times, people who have been burnt in the past in their relationships use this as an excuse for not wanting to be in a relationship. They will be like, "I'm done. I had enough of the games people play and getting hurt. Blah blah blah. Let's face it, we've all gotten our hearts broken once, twice, or maybe even more. Does that mean we should never pursue another relationship again? No. It is like falling off a horse. Does that mean we aren't gonna get back up on that horse again? No. We will get back up on that horse and ride it again. Well the same thing goes for relationships. Get out there and mingle. Be brave, move forward, and take a chance. Who knows, the next person you are taking a chance on could be your soul mate.

Love and trust take time. If there is anything I've learned through my experiences, it would be to give people the benefit of the doubt. When we jump into conclusions, we could be missing out on something great. Don't overanalyze or put things into your head that are not happening. Overthinking causes us to worry for no reason at all. Just go with the flow, and be happy. Most importantly, do not be afraid to love again. Let love find you. It found me.

Chapter 8

GROWING AS A PERSON

When we were little, we wanted to be adults. We thought it would be so much fun being an adult. There would be no rules to follow. We could come home whenever we wanted and do whatever we wanted to do. We would watch our parents' every move and try to copy it because we wanted to be older and wiser like them.

If you were like me, you played house. I played house with my cousin Tina who, by the way, is more like a sister to me. Shanna, our sweet friend, lived next door to us when we were younger. She played house with us too.

She passed away from breast cancer two years ago. She was only thirty-nine years old. We were all very close in our younger years. We had Cabbage Patch Kids. We pretended they were our kids. We thought playing house was fun, and we couldn't wait to grow up. Little did we know, it was easier being a kid. As we grew up, we realized adulthood was not what it was cracked up to be. We realized there were bills to be paid, responsibilities, work. and etc. We began to wish we were kids again.

Today, kids want to grow up too fast.

At the age of thirteen, kids have boyfriends or girlfriends, while at that age, I was still playing house, playing with dolls, and had no interest in boys. Times sure have changed. I'm happy I grew up in a time like I did.

Looking back on the good old days, there are a few things I would have changed. But I'm also grateful for it all.

As we grow up, we learn that age brings wisdom. Being an adult isn't all that bad. Life is what we make it. We have choices. We can either be miserable or make ourselves happy. I don't know about you, but I love being happy. Why be miserable? You just bring everyone else around you down.

God wants us to be happy. In scripture, Psalm 37:4 reads, "Take delight in the Lord, and he will give you desires of your heart."

And Psalm 126:2 says, "Our mouths were filled with laughter, our tongues with songs of joy." In fact, God tells us more times in the Scripture to be happy than any other command. Think about that! Commands such as "rejoice," "be of good cheer," "do not be afraid," "give thanks" are all different ways of God telling us to be happy. Wow, isn't that powerful? The devil, on the other hand—well let's just say—wants the opposite.

As we get older, we realize what's important and what's not. We realize how much we need God. It is never too late to find God and walk beside him.

Growing up, I didn't have a church life. We didn't go to church much at all, but I knew God existed. I always believed in God, but my faith has grown so much in the last five years. You see, God led me to an awesome, inspiring church called Cornerstone located in Oxford, Connecticut. It has allowed me to deepen my faith and my walk with God. I was actually water baptized at Cornerstone Church. It was an awesome experience. In case you don't know what water baptism is, it is a public declaration of our faith in Jesus Christ and the outward demonstration of the inward transformation that takes place when we receive him as our Lord and Savior. It is a way of us saying goodbye to our old life and saying hello to our new life. The reason I got water baptized was because I wanted to help inspire others, be closer to Jesus, be secure within my inner self, and to live life without anxiety. If you never been water baptized, I would encourage you to do it. It is amazing.

What is true happiness? The Bible tells us that the only source of true joy and happiness is in God. Our obedience to God brings true happiness. Putting Him above us is where happiness is found. Jesus stated in the popular Bible verse of Matthew 22:37, "Love the Lord your God with all your heart and with all your soul and with all your mind." And who better leads by example than God in the ultimate sacrificial Bible verse on love? "For God so loved the world that he gave his one and only Son." How powerful and true that is.

When we learn how to transition from our old ways and transition into our new ways, life begins to have more meaning. We can't do this without the help from God. When we put our trust and faith in God, when we open our hearts up to the Lord, that is when we will see a change in our lives—how we think and react to things. I am not saying there won't be trials and errors. What I will say when those trials and errors come along is that it'll be easier for you to take them on. It'll be easier to take them out because you have let God into your life to take control of every given situation you are facing. I don't know about you, but I love my new way of life.

I love how much I've grown in my faith. I give all the thanks in the world to God. If it weren't for him, I would not be where I am today. I thank him for showing me how to live a much better and happier life. Do you want to know how my faith grew? Great, I'm happy you asked.

Actually, it is really quite simple, although it didn't happen overnight. Just like anything, things take time. It happened over the years.

You see, I got sick and tired of living a life full of insecurities. I had trust issues. I would question things. I would analyze every given situation. I had a failed relationship because of it. Because who wants to be questioned over things repeatedly? Who wants to feel like the other person they are with does not trust them? Nobody does, right? If I had God in my life back then, things probably would have been different. But we all know we cannot change what happened already. All we can do is live by mistakes and move forward.

Then that's when it all happened, and life began to get better because I let God in. I turned to God for help. I let God take control over my life, and I let him take control of the wheel. I was just sick and tired of living my life this way. I'm not saying I still don't get insecure, but what I will say is it has gotten a lot better. If I can reach out and let God in, so can you.

The reason for my insecurities and overanalyzing things was due to anxiety, which I never even knew it was related to anxiety until I went to the doctor. It got so bad that I felt like I was having a nervous breakdown when I was at work three years ago. I felt God led me to the doctor. to get the help I needed. You see, I always knew anxiety had to do with a nervous feeling, feeling closed in, and anxious; but I never knew about the other issues that happen with it. There are other types of anxiety that I will be covering in another chapter.

We all go through things in life. We all make mistakes. But if we don't learn from them, we will go on making the same mistakes. Mistakes are going to happen. That's why there are erasers on pencils. After all, we are human. Nobody is perfect, so therefore mistakes will happen. Besides, making mistakes is how we grow as a person and how we learn.

When we grow as a person, our life becomes greater and better. But what does it mean to grow as a person? Let's take a look at what it means.

Growing as a person is to grow in areas that make us a better person. When we have good morals, we grow as a person. When we say that someone "grows as a person," we mean that the person has grown emotionally and mentally. They recognize and understand things they did not know before.

This can happen through the acquisition of knowledge or simply through experiences in life. For example, "She has been through a lot of rough times, but this has made her grow as a person." Another example of growing as a person is taking responsibility and accountability for our actions. We apologize first even when we are not the ones at fault. This just means we are being the better person and doing the right thing. We don't seek revenge when someone does us wrong. We let our God take care of it.

Self-growth is beautiful. Self-growth is a lifelong process, but it is something that happens every day even though we may not notice it at the moment.

However, if you can take a second to self-reflect on the person you are today, look back at yourself five years ago. Is the growth you see amazing? It should be. If not, I will list ways that will help you feel better about who you are.

But first, let me just share this: When I reflect back on who I was three years ago and now, I'd say I'm stronger, less insecure, a better person, more caring, outgoing, and funny. I laugh and joke around more. I am aware of my mistakes. I am imperfect, but I've always known this (haha).

Even though I see how far I've come, there are still things I have to work on within myself. I'm fine with this because there will always be things we will find that we have to improve about ourselves. That's why it is called growing as a person.

In the next few paragraphs, I'll go over thirteen ways that have helped me grow as a person. I pray that they will be a help to you.

1. Love yourself. One of the hardest tasks we may ever face is self-love and appreciation. However, this is the most important thing you need to get through life. You must love yourself. Once you learn to love yourself, you can love others and life a whole lot more. One way to do this is to look at yourself in the mirror every day and be happy with the reflection that you see because you are awesome.

2. Forgive. Forgiveness is a lot easier said than done. However, forgiveness brings you inner peace and helps set you free. It can be challenging, but letting go of angry thoughts and resentment will help you to grow into a stronger person in the end. Bitterness just grows into more hatred. Life is not long enough to keep living it this way. In the end, you are only hurting yourself.

3. Stand your ground. If you're like me, you probably weren't born with the natural power to speak up for yourself when the situation calls for it. It took me years before I was able to do this because I was afraid of overstepping my ground. Now I will just say how I feel, although I do it in a respectable manner. Standing your ground, whether it be in regard

to an unpopular opinion or when someone is doing you wrong, is what shapes your personality into a mature and strong adult. When you finally give yourself the power to speak up, you will feel like a brand-new person.

4. Figure out what you like. See what your favorite movie is, and figure out why it's your favorite movie. Learn your own political view and religious choices. Analyze your favorite type of music. Do not let anyone else decide these things for you. Don't like something just because someone else likes it. You have to be your own person. To do this, you must figure out what it is that you like or don't like.

5. Let new people into your life. It's hard to make new relationships, whether it be romance, friendship, or just getting along with coworkers. But think about all of those who have come into your life in the past few years that really mean a lot to you. If you had never let them into your life, you wouldn't have that special relationship to cherish. You never know when the next person you meet might change your life. Always keep in mind, just because others may have betrayed your trust, doesn't mean the next person will. I always give people the benefit of the doubt. Sometimes it isn't easy, but we have to start from somewhere, right?

6. Don't be afraid to be yourself. Everyone is persuading you to be a certain person: your society, your family, and your friends. They can try all they want; but at the end of the day, you have to be you. If people do not like the real you, that's on them. Never be afraid to be who you truly are. You have to be your own person and not a copycat of someone else. Don't compare yourself to others. Run your own race. If we look at what others are doing, then we will never succeed in the goals we set out for ourselves.

7. Discover new things. Take a road trip, try new food, or read a new book. The world has so much to offer. If you discover new things, you might discover more about what you like and, in turn, discover more about who you are. Self-growth is shaped by knowing who you are as an individual.

8. Keep people in your life that you need. Learn who is bringing positivity and growth to you as a person, and keep them around. Learn who is bringing you down, and kick them to the curb. The people you put yourself around will impact you. So in order to grow, you need people in your life who are right for you. Once you realize negative people bring you down, you won't want this type of energy around you. You'll be happy it escaped you because positive energy is so much rewarding.

9. Take responsibility for your actions. This one is tough. It can be so difficult to admit to others that you have messed up. Some individuals never learn how to do this. But knowing what you've done wrong and admitting to it, especially admitting it to yourself, is humbling and helps you learn how to not make the same mistakes again. This, my friends, helps you grow as a person.

10. Listen to your own instincts. If you feel something in your heart, you need to listen to it. Just because what you feel isn't in statistical data doesn't mean it can't be real. Your instincts are ingrained in you because they help you to know how to survive. Don't ignore them. I wish I had listened to mine because it would have prevented some heartbreaks.

11. Set your goals high. Make sure your goals are realistic, but push yourself further than you think you can go. If you set goals you know for sure you can achieve, you've set the bar too low. Do things that are risky or put fear into you. Set goals that you are unsure of and need to work very hard to reach. Once you reach them, you will feel much better about yourself. Like I've stated before, and probably will again, run your own race. Don't look at what the other person is doing. If you do, you will be stuck in the same spot you started a year ago. Go live out your dreams, not the dreams somebody else wants for you.

12. Know your strengths and weaknesses. No one is perfect. Some people are better at certain things than others. You have to admit that you might not be good at painting, soc-

cer, or public speaking. However, you also need to admit when you are good at something. Maybe you are the best singer, the best at giving advice, or the best makeup artist. If you don't admit that these are your strengths, you are wasting them and not showing them to the world. Most importantly, you are not growing as a person if you keep these talents hidden.

13. Lastly, reflect on who you are. Self-reflection is something that many people like to avoid because they are worried about what they can find, but you need to know who you are deep inside. There is a part of you that no other person knows except for you. In order to know who you are and who you want to show the world, you have to look inside yourself and ask, "Who am I?"

Most importantly, never be afraid to be who you are. Don't worry about what people think and say about you. Personally, it is none of your business. All that does is hold you back from what God has set out for you to do. If you worry about what others think of you, in years to come, you will have regrets you didn't do what you wanted to do because you worried about what others thought of you. This goes for listening to what others tell you not to do as well. If you don't do what is right for you, you will have regrets later on in life.

When I was little, my mom would tell me to never give up. She would say giving up was for cowards. I've learned a lot from my mom—how to love, care for others, be honest, be loyal, and so much more. My mother was the kindest, most good-hearted, and caring woman you would ever like to meet. Losing her at a young age of nineteen was not easy. She passed away unexpectedly from a heart attack at the age of fifty-three. Although it was the worst night of my life, I can feel her spirit around me. I can feel her guiding me along.in my life's journey. My mom passing on into heaven changed my life, but it also made me stronger.

Don't get me wrong, it was hard when my mom passed on. I would cry continuously. I would cry because I lost my best friend, my mom. No matter what I did, I felt I was not good enough. I felt

I wasn't smart enough. After a while, I did get confidence because I would remember my mom's positive words sinking into my brain. "Get up, my daughter. You are smart, wise, not a quitter, and courageous." Those words stick with me.

Looking back now and little did I know, it was God who was working in me and helping me to move forward in my life's journey. It was God who was making me remember what my mom said.

You see, we are given two options in life: We can either live life bitter when someone we love passes on, or we can live a life full of possibilities and happiness. I choose to live a life full of possibilities and happiness because that is what our loved ones would want for us. They don't want us moping around, being sad. They want us to live the rest of our lives happy.

Don't get me wrong, it is okay to grieve and be sad, but there comes a time when we have to let go and move on. That doesn't mean we don't miss our loved ones, or we won't cry from time to time. That is not what I'm saying. But what I am saying is we can't go through life in pain, filled with hatred and sadness because that gets us nowhere. It just brings on more depression and anxiety. God wants us to live life happy and not sad because he is a good Father. It is the enemy who wants us to live life in sadness and everything else that does not blossom into the good positive fruit of goodness.

When we grow as a person, we learn from our parents, teachers, friends, and others. I've learned a lot from my mom, like I've said before.

She was so compassionate. She could talk to anyone. I remember being in the store with my mom, and she could start up a conversation with a stranger and anyone she met. It was so great seeing this. She rubbed off on me because I'm like my mom. She was such a positive, happy person. I could talk to her about anything. She was just a super loving mom and the best mom I could ever have.

I thank God for choosing her to be my mom. She brought so much beauty into the world. Losing her at a young age made me a stronger and better person. Sometimes I try to imagine how life would be if she were still physically here. She would still be wearing her funky clothes and earrings I'm sure (haha). By the way, they looked great on her, and she could pull it off. My family says I'm just like my mom. It never gets old hearing this. She is in heaven, but I can feel her guiding me so I can live my best life here on earth. Amen to that!

Growing as a person is a process. It is a process that never ends because we are always growing and learning. They say that God doesn't give us more than we can handle, and I find this to be true. He is always testing our strengths and guiding us along the way. Let's face it, if everything in life ran smooth all the time, then we wouldn't have challenges. Challenges make us stronger and better. When the good and the not so good happen to us, it brings out our strong points.

When we grow as a person, we realize it is not about how many friends we have in our lives that matters. It is about those that are in our lives who are willing to stay that matters. It is also about having friends who are there for you in the good and not so good times. Friends who are loyal, true, real, and who will never betray you are the ones you want in your life. If you do not have friends that are like this, then it is time to let them go.

Chapter 9

BEING STRONG
AND WEAK

Even though my mom's passing made me a stronger person, there have been bumps in the road that occurred. I went through a rough time in my life where I wasn't always so positive, happy, and secure as I am today. A lot had to do with anxiety. I didn't realize all the symptoms that came with anxiety like I do today. If I had, my life would have been a little different. I believe God has us go through things so we can help others who may be going through the same thing we went through.

I will talk more about anxiety in another chapter. For now, I will say it is not as easy as putting anxiety in a box and hiding it away. Some people say, "Think positive, and anxiety will go away." If it were all that easy, then nobody would have it.

I was in a dark place in my life. I had trouble trusting others. I was paranoid with thinking everyone was against me. The insecurities that I had, though, made me stronger. All this stemmed from anxiety that I was unaware of.

I thank God for all he has done for me all the time. I am where I am today from praying and talking to God.

There are times when I'm strong, but there are also times when I'm weak. This is normal. Let's face it, we are humans, so this will happen. In the next paragraph, I'll give you an example of how I felt defeated.

For instance, I had bunion surgery on September 9, 2020 on my right foot and then on my left foot on January 27, 2021. The same doctor did both feet. Little did I know there were complications with my two feet that were operated on. So on April 2021, I went and got a second opinion by a different doctor. I was referred to go to him by a family friend named Dicky. He knows someone that went to that doctor to have bunion surgery and it ended up being successful.

Well the doctor told me that I had to have bunion revision surgery. He said the bunion was still there. After hearing this, I felt defeated. I felt like crying. I actually was starting to when he told me the bad news when I was in the office. I was like, I just had this done, and I did everything the doctor told me to do the first and second time around. I had to be out of work for three weeks for the right foot and two weeks for the second foot.

The doctor had to put an external fixator device in my foot during surgery. He had to put this in to keep my toe straight and for the bone to grow and heal properly. If I had gone to him from the beginning, this would not have taken place; and there would have been no downtime. But it is what it is. That will have to come out when the time comes. I'll have to go to the OR to have it taken out, but there is no downtime with it, which is great!

The great thing was that I was able to work on my book. If there was anything good that came out of the ordeal, it was that I was able to focus on getting my book done. Because let's face it, when we are working and such, it is hard to fit other things in that we want to get done.

Oh, and the other good news was my foot was healing; and I'd be going to therapy on June 17, 2021. I was very excited.

I wasn't going to talk about my foot surgery, but I want people to be more mindful and do their research when having any kind of surgery done. Don't just do the research, but go get different opinions from different doctors. Don't have it done by the first doctor you go to like I did. Go and get opinions, take notes, and ask a lot of questions. Like anything in life, this was a lesson to be learned.

I will have to have the left foot done the same way that I had the right foot done.

Reflecting back as to what I have stated before, I would never seek revenge. I'm not saying I wasn't bitter by what happened. I was bitter because of having to go through this all over again and having to be out of work for so long. I am sure the other doctor that didn't do my foot operation correctly did not seek out to do me wrong. He just was not competent. But God will take care of the situation just like he helped me find a great doctor to fix it. I'm very grateful for that. I just pray that this doesn't happen to anyone else.

As we grow, we can read people. We know what their motives are, who we can trust and who we can't, who is being honest and who isn't. I believe God helps us with this as well.

He puts stopblocks in people's way to prevent them from causing us hurt and pain. Sometimes we overlook God's voice without even realizing we are, or we don't obey what he is trying to warn us not to do and who we should stay away from. We think we don't need God because we can handle it on our own. It is a big mistake to think that because, let me just say, I would not be where I am today if it weren't for God. He is a good father, and he eventually leads us to the truth. We may be weak at first to overcome the hurt, but God helps us get stronger.

Some of us know what we want out of life. Some of us have it all figured out. Having an education is more important than having a relationship. I honestly wish I put education before anything in my younger years rather than trying to find a great guy to settle down with. Don't get me wrong, I love my life, but I just wish back then that I had taken control over my life a little more. It would have helped if I had it all figured out back then. I would have put education first, then relationship, marriage, and then who knows? I may have had kids. But life is too short to live with regrets.

Looking back now, I believe things happen the way they are meant to happen. In the end, I believe God will lead us to where we are meant to be. I've learned that even though we may not have our life figured out, say, by the time we are twenty, eventually we will. Some think that if they don't have their life figured out by a certain age, then they never will.

I'm here to say, that is far from the truth. Some of us change careers at a later age. We start out working at something that we went to college for; but then we realize that what we went to college for, we don't want to do. It isn't always easy knowing what we want to do while we are in college because it sounds good, and it sounds like something we want to do. But when we go into the working world to do it, we realize it is not what we want to be doing.

We may feel weak telling our parents this because, after all, some of us had help with paying for it. While it may be hard to tell our parents about our career change, it also makes us stronger by coming forward about it. It takes the pressure off of us. Because let's face it, nobody wants to work somewhere that they really don't want to work at.

I've changed careers a few times. It is like I said before, we go to school for something, then we realize that it isn't what we thought it was going to be. Well that's what happened to me. I went to college for a couple of years, on and off, for art; but then I didn't like the art program offered at Naugatuck Community Technical College located in Waterbury Connecticut, so I stopped going. I did get financial aid for that, so that was awesome.

Then I went on and worked at Griffin Hospital. I worked there for five years in the central processing department. It was an on-the-job training, so I didn't have to go to school for it. It involved cleaning the doctors' tools that they used for surgeries. It was a big and important job because without that department, the hospital can't operate. It was not just cleaning the doctors' tools but also sterilizing them, preparing the surgical carts, lifting heavy equipment, and putting the right tools in the sets to be sterilized in these big autoclaves. This job came with big responsibilities, and of course, we didn't make what we should have been making. I loved it at first, but then it became stressful. It became stressful because they added more and more things for us to do.

So then I decided to go to school for CNA (certified nurse aide). I wanted to stay working in the medical field, so I decided to go to school for CNA. While I was in school, I still worked at Griffin in the same department. I had to work while going to school because I needed to make money. It was a six-month course taught at St. Vincent's Hospital in Bridgeport, Connecticut. I actually did a little more than CNA.

What I actually went to school for was multiskilled tech, which consisted of phlebotomy, CNA, and EKG. When they call it multi-, they mean you are doing more than one thing.

I did great in school, and I liked it. I graduated. But when it came time to work in the hospital to do it, I didn't like it too much. See, I told you I went to school for something, then it turned out I didn't like it. I shouldn't say I didn't like it. It's just that the hospital put too much on us that they wanted us to do.

I don't mind being busy and working, but it was just overwhelming. I was a float, so I never knew where I was going to be working in the hospital, which did not make things any easier.

I remember my instructor saying that one week we would be drawing blood; then the next week, we would be doing EKG; and another week, we would be doing CNA work. Well that was not the case because we were doing all that in one day.

If you worked on the floors, you had to go into the patients' rooms to do vital signs. Then once those were done, you had to go back in the patients' rooms to draw their blood for whatever blood work the doctor needed it for then enter all the information into the computer for the blood work. Then would you get your assignment for patients who you had to wash up in bed. There would be six patients that you had to wash up. On top of doing all that, you had to answer call lights, check on the patients, and if there were any patients who needed help feeding, you had to do that too. Oh, and you had to do EKG if there were orders to do them.

Don't get me wrong, I love to be busy and to work, but that was way too much. At least I thought so. I look at it this way: We were taking care of patients, we should not have to be rushing around like that. To me, that was where mistakes took place. So needless to say, I worked as a multiskilled tech for six months.

Then I went on and worked as a CNA at the Visiting Nurse Services in Oxford, Connecticut. I went to patients' houses to help them take showers and do some light housework, like doing the laundry and changing their bed linens. I liked this better because we had one-on-one with the patients. I worked there for eight years, then I wanted to do something else.

So while working as a CNA at the Visiting Nurse Services, I went to school for hairdressing.

Fast forward, ten years later, I still love what I do.

You see, we may have to take different roads in life to get where we want to work. I believe this is my calling.

It may be scary trying something new; but in the end, it is worth it.

When I would take my gram to get her hair done at the salon, I knew I wanted to be a hairstylist. The only problem with that was I could never find a school that offered financial aid. I needed some kind of aid because there was no way I could afford to pay all the money upfront.

So then one day, it happened. I had the opportunity to go to a hairdressing school in Oxford, Connecticut, called Oxford Hair Academy of Cosmetology School. That was the year of 2009 in October. It was the best decision that I made.

The school at the time was walking distance from my house. Then before I graduated, they moved to Seymour, a town over, because the school began to expand. I was able to get $5,000 in aid, and I was able to pay the rest when I graduated, which was like $10,000. I didn't have to pay it all at once. I was able to make payments, which was awesome. I believe I paid it off six years later. I loved the school. I would definitely recommend others to go there.

I became a hairstylist at the age of thirty-five. Like I said, fast forward to ten years, I still love what I do. It doesn't matter how old we are, it is never too late to do something new.

Although I loved the fact I was going to hairdressing school, I had my struggles when it came time to learn. Nothing comes easy for me when it comes to learning something new.

I always felt like there was something wrong with me. I felt defeated, weak, and like I was never going to catch on when it came to hairdressing. Everyone else seemed to get the hang of how to do hair but me. As I caught on, I realized there was nothing wrong with me, it just took me time to learn. I graduated with honors. A scripture that I love is this: I can do all things through God who gives me strength (Philippians 4:13).

Looking back now, I realize that everyone learns differently, and some people just catch on quicker than others. Just because someone is a quick learner doesn't mean that person is smarter than the other person. Don't ever say you are not smart, or you can't do something. Those are the enemy's lies telling you that. God, on the other hand, is telling you that you are smart and that you will achieve your goals.

When it comes to learning, I'm hands on. I can read and read something. It'll make sense. But for me, to learn is hands on.

When we feel weak, we think we are not strong enough to move forward when something traumatic happens to us, whether it be a divorce, breakup, death, friends' betrayal, failure in class or test, and so forth, which is farther from the truth. Sometimes, some of us are too hard on ourselves. Life is not always smooth sailing. There will be times in our lives when things will bring us down. We will have a hard time coping with things; but this doesn't mean we are weak; it just means we have weak moments. This is a natural way to feel. Hey, let's face it, we are humans.

Life is beautiful. There are good things and not-so-good things that happen. When something as bad as a hurricane or tornado happens, it brings tragedy sometimes.

Our house may had been ruined from trees that had fallen on it, or our car may had been damaged. There might had been so many trees that had fallen, and now you would have to pay a lot of money to get someone to get rid of them. At that very moment, we might had felt defeated and thought things would never get better. All we wanted to do was crawl in a hole and not come out. But when we look back a year from when it happened, we realize we were stronger than we thought we could ever be. God had brought you through that, and he will continue to bring you through whatever turmoil you may face. Isaiah 41:10 reads, "So do not fear, for I am with you; do not be dismayed, for I am your God. I will strengthen you and help you; I will uphold you with my righteous hand." Now that is powerful and brings great comfort and meaning. Another scripture I love is this Isaiah 40:31: But those who hope in the Lord will renew their strength. They will soar on wings like eagles; they will run and not grow weary; they will walk and not be faint.

And another one is Psalm 73:26: "My flesh and my heart may fail, but God is the strength of my heart and my portion forever."

Amen. Amen.

Maybe you are struggling with your finances, or your house went into foreclosure. You feel like things won't get better. It is so easy to feel defeated and anxious. But can I just say, we serve the most powerful God who will bring you through. When something bad happens, I believe it happens for the better so something great can happen.

God doesn't cause bad things to happen. People do. Let's face it, we live in a world that is filled with evil. I always say, if people have more God in their lives, then evil things won't happen.

When a marriage or relationship doesn't work out, it just means you are made to be with someone else. I don't say failed marriage or relationship because there is no such thing as failing. We grow and learn to do things better.

Maybe the person you were once with didn't treat you right. Maybe your marriage/relationship was filled with dishonesty, physical and/or mental abuse, betrayal, and nothing good that came with it. You couldn't see your way out. You didn't think things would get better. Or maybe you just couldn't see the wrong things that the other person was doing to you, but others could. When we are in a situation, we don't realize how bad it is until we are away from the situation we were once in. Let me just say, you may not have felt strong enough to pray, but someone else was praying over you. Because someone else prayed for you, you were able to get out of that situation you were once in, and you got through it. God is always good, and He wants us all to live happy and healthy lives.

I wasn't always so secure. I had insecurity issues. When I was younger, I used to think I something was wrong with me because I got picked on in high school. I used to think I wasn't good enough.

I would want a man to make me happy. I would want a man to make me feel good about myself because I was insecure within myself. I would want a man to give me compliments just so I would feel good about myself.

As I grew up, all that changed. I began to get confidence and felt secure within myself.

I no longer looked for a man to make me happy or to make me feel good about who I was. I began to make myself happy. In order to be loved, we must learn to love ourselves before another can.

When we have a big test to take in school, driving school, or any other type of test, sometimes we put so much fear and pressure on ourselves that we begin to think we will fail it. We put ourselves up for failure even before we take the test. When the test results come back, you find that you did awesome and that you worried for nothing.

The moral of the story is to take a deep breath and pray because, in the end, you'll do great. Have confidence in yourself, and worry less because you are awesome.

Chapter 10

TAKING CHANCES

In order to get ahead in life and succeed, we must learn how to take chances.

We need to learn how to get out of our comfort zone, which is not always easy. We let fear hold us back. We listen to our inner voice that says, "I can't do that. What if I fail?" How about saying, "What if I do amazing? Oh, and I can do that." All it takes is reprogramming our thoughts, and the rest will fall into place.

I remember selling Mary Kay. I was my best customer (me laughing). I didn't succeed in it, but I also did not fail at it. Sometimes, things don't work out. The main thing is that I tried it, and I learned it was not my calling. In order to know if something is for us, we need to try it. I don't look at it as a waste of time because I learned from it. I have no regrets with trying to give it a go. Not everything is for everyone; but if we don't try different things, how will we ever know if it is for us or not?

Keep in mind that just because someone is succeeding at something that you are not doesn't mean you are not smart. It just means you either have to work harder at it, or it's not for you. Not everyone can do what the other person can do. That's why some are nurses, doctors, teachers, hairdressers, veterinarians, and so on. We all have things we are good at that someone else may not be good at. We all have our own niche in life. God made us all unique and gave us all different talents. He wants us all to live out the talent he gave us. If we don't use the talents God gave us, then what good is it? It's like buying a car and not driving it.

When I was a CNA, I knew I didn't want to be a nurse. Not that I couldn't do it, but I just knew that was not what I wanted to do. It wasn't my calling. And if I'm being honest, I'm not the college type.

My cousin Tina, on the other hand, became a CNA and then went on to be a nurse. She's an excellent nurse if I must say. Like I said, we all have our calling in life.

In school comes pure pressure, and kids want to be like other kids. Kids want what their friends have. Kids feel that if they don't do what their friends do, then they are just not cool. Parents should be teaching their kids to be themselves and not like another. Be the leader and not the follower. It takes a strong-minded person to lead his/her way. It's not always easy living in the younger generation where you are trying to find yourself and where you fit in. Heck, as an adult, we are still trying to figure it all out.

I believe, throughout our lives, we are always learning, whether it be about ourselves, from others, work, life, and etc.

I was that girl who was always worried about what others thought about me. As I got older, that changed.

I feel for the kids that worry about what other kids think and say about them. High school is supposed to be the best years of their life. Kids shouldn't have to worry about fitting in, what clothes others are wearing, hairstyles etc. They should be concentrating on their studies and making friends. They should be able to be their own person. I feel that if schools taught this, then there would be less bullying. If schools taught more about taking chances, then kids wouldn't be so afraid to try something different. They would be able to get out of their comfort zones.

I was once like this when I was in school. I was shy, insecure, and like I said before, I cared what others thought and said about me. It was not the best way to live or be. As I got older, and I put it all in God's hands, it all changed. When we turn our problems over to God, that is when we see change, growth, and peace.

I was weak, but God made me strong.

As I type up my book, I can't believe it has been five years since I've been working on it. Today is June 11, 2021. I haven't been consistent with it, so that's why it is not complete yet. Let's face it, life happens, and I didn't get a chance to work on it. I always say, it doesn't matter how long something takes us to complete it. What matters is that we do it.

I know I just got off track with my book, but I just wanted to include how long I've been working on my book.

I talk about my school days in hopes it will help others that are getting bullied. I dislike it when I hear that others get bullied. Being a kid isn't easy. Between the peer pressure and kids worrying about fitting in, it makes it a bit challenging.

As we mature into adults, we may never get over being insecure or stop worrying about what others think of us and what others are saying about us. But if we don't take the chance and say, "I'm not going to care anymore about what others are saying and thinking of me," then we will never break the cycle. What has gotten me through this was saying it is none of my business what people are saying about me. It is none of my business what people think of me.

Furthermore, I honestly don't care what others think and say about me because I know God already approves me and loves me. You too should have this mindset because God wants us all to be happy, and He does not want this kind of pressure put on us. The more we take chances and do things, the easier it will be. It's like this: The more we do something, the better we become at it. Amen.

Chapter 11

BOUNDARIES

B oundaries—hmm, what are they? Many people have the wrong idea about boundaries. They believe that they already have good boundaries, when in reality, they have brick walls, or they believe that boundaries are "unkind."

Healthy boundaries are the ultimate guide to successful relationships. Without healthy boundaries, relationships do not thrive. They result in feelings of resentment, disappointment, or violation. These feelings, if unchecked, can lead to being cut off from others or enmeshment, where there's no clear division between you and others' needs and feelings. Neither of these situations is ideal. Because so few of us understand what boundaries actually are, we rarely see evidence of them working. But when they do, you feel it. It does wonders for your mental and relational health.

What does healthy boundaries look like?

Boundaries are what happen when you can sense yourself, what you need and want, and access your voice to speak to those things. We all have "limits," and we all experience violations of our limits.

Most of the time, people are not trying to violate your limits, they just aren't aware of what they are. Sometimes, this is because we are not clear with ourselves or other people about what we want or need.

We all need time apart from the world. It's normal to feel like this. Between work, home life, etc., it all has a way of catching up with us.

Sometimes people overstep our space and want things done when they want them done. We feel guilty if we don't give a helping hand. So saying no is not an option. Sometimes though, we have to learn how to say no; otherwise people will take advantage of us. I know it's not always easy saying no because I'm still learning this myself. We don't want to say no because we don't want the other person to get mad at us. This is how I am too. I'm not saying I don't want to help when it's needed; but let's face it, we are human and we need our down time too.

Everything happens in moderation. Sometimes, learning how to set boundaries happens in moderation as well.

I've learned that prying into people's lives could be crossing the line a bit. If someone doesn't want to tell us something that's going on in their life, we have to learn to accept it and not pry into their life. If someone wants us to know something, they'll tell us freely themselves. If someone doesn't want to talk about something that is bothering them, then we have to be respectful. These are all boundaries that we have to learn not to cross.

Love can't exist if there are no boundaries. This goes for when we have children, pets, in our marriages, relationships, etc.

Saying no to your children when they want something isn't always easy. They are oh so cute; so saying no to their cute little faces is oh so hard at times, isn't it? But if we want them to grow and learn boundaries, then we have to learn how to say no.

There are many types of boundaries, and the art of learning them takes time. It has taken me time to learn this, and I'm still learning this. Heck, we learn every day.

Some of the boundaries I'm going to tell you about are as follows: material, physical, mental, emotional, spiritual, and I'm sure there are more.

The first one I'm going to tell you about is material boundaries.

Material boundaries are knowing when it is okay to give or lend things to someone. These things might be food, money, cars, clothes, etc. It's okay to want to help, but overstepping the giving isn't okay.

People tend to take advantage of your kindness if you give too much. One way you can make sure this doesn't happen is by not being overly nice. It's okay to be nice; but when people see your kindheartedness, they can easily take advantage of you without you even realizing it. God loves when we help one another; but what he doesn't approve of is when we take advantage of people.

The next boundary I'm going to tell you about is the physical boundary. This pertains to your personal space, privacy, and body. You have every right to stop someone who's overstepping your space. This may apply if someone is pressuring you into sex, and you aren't wanting no part of it. It is your right and your body to say no. That person should respect you. And if not, there will be consequences for that person's actions. Another example of physical boundaries is someone who is snooping into your personal belongings, like your diary, email, social media accounts, phone, etc. Some people think they have the right to your personal space, but they obviously do not. Nobody has the right to invade someone else's personal business. This is why it is so important to practice boundaries. The old saying goes: Don't do to others what you don't want done to you, but do to others what you would want done to you. Amen.

Another boundary I'm going to tell you about is mental boundaries. This applies to your thoughts, values, and opinions. We all have different opinions about things. We may not always agree on the same things, but that's just human nature. We aren't made to agree with one another all the time. Be courteous to someone else who has their own opinion about something. We all think differently and have different views on things. Someone may not like the president while somebody else does, so be respectful, and don't say mean things to one another. Be respectful at all times. Someone may think the picture on the wall looks ridiculous. While another may think it looks beautiful. We all have different tastes and likings.

We all value different things. This could be a purse, book, pen, Bible, etc. Whatever it is that brings you value, go for it. Just because you don't find it valuable and somebody else does, it doesn't give anyone the right to judge someone. So be respectful.

The other boundary I'm going to tell you about is emotional boundaries. Emotional boundaries are crucial in helping us to enjoy healthy relationships and to avoid unhealthy or dysfunctional ones. Unhealthy boundaries are ones where we are secretive, or we avoid being hurt, so we don't get close to people.

There are also strong and healthy emotional boundaries. They are not based on arrogance and fear. Strong and healthy emotional boundaries can be quite transparent. Well it's more like a wire fence. People can see through it if they like, but that doesn't mean they can come in.

These boundaries keep us strong, safe, and happy. It's a sign of self-care and self-respect. We shall all have these types of boundaries.

When we have a strong conception of our own identity, we do not feel threatened by the intimacy of the relationship we are in. We can appreciate and love those qualities in our partner that make her/him unique.

A successful relationship is composed of two individuals, each with his/her own identity. When we have a strongly built foundation, the relationship we are in will continue to blossom.

Self-love is so important. If you don't have this, the relationship you are in will sink. You need to figure out what you want in the relationship you are in. This is why emotional boundaries are important.

Emotional boundaries don't just apply to relationships/marriages, they also apply to friendships and family. It is very important to have a firm foundation in them as well.

The last boundary I'm going to talk about is spiritual boundaries. To have strong spiritual boundaries, we have to figure out what our beliefs are. We have to figure it out on our own. This means that we should not listen to others when they try to tell us what to believe in. We should not force religion on others because all that does is bring resentment.

I believe in God 100 percent because he has done so much in my life. He has brought me out of darkness and has guided me to see the light on things. God has helped me get through heartache, grief for the loss of loved ones, difficulties with learning, trusting, anxiety, and so much more. He is a good Father. But just because I believe in God does not mean I'm going to force people to believe in him. I can tell you one thing though: I will never stop talking about God when I'm around others because he is real and lives inside all of us. I believe everyone has to find their way and follow their heart on the matter. Regardless, God loves us, and he will lead people to him. The only thing I can do is pray over people that they turn to God; because if they don't, then their life will continue to be empty and be filled with darkness.

If we are going to let God into our lives, then we need to learn how to have strong spiritual boundaries.

Our choice of friends is important in our spiritual walk. The Bible gives us guidance about the type of person we should be seeking as a friend. Our close friends should exhibit godly wisdom and shall love God too. We shouldn't make friends with those who are easily tempered and get angry easily. We should choose friends who make good and not bad choices. How your friends treat others says a lot about their character. Our close friends should be willing to tell us the truth even when it hurts.

Nobody has the right to judge someone's spirituality. We all have our own beliefs. If someone is judging you, then do yourself a favor and just walk away. It does no good to try and defend yourself because all that does is add more fuel to the fire. You owe nobody an explanation, nor do you have to justify yourself.

If we don't know what spiritual boundaries are, then it will just lead to a lot of aggravation, pain, and hardship.

My strong spiritual boundaries come from my strong faith that I set out for myself. I don't care what people think of my faith and beliefs. To be honest, this is how we all should feel and be. Because my faith is awesome, I don't get turned away by people's negativity. Instead, I stay positive. God is working in me; so with that, it just makes me be more positive. Some people need positivity in their lives, so I believe God has me working through him to help them. I also believe he has others working through him to help other people as well. I walk in faith because life isn't long enough not to.

When we hang around bitter people who are judgmental, mean, and the not-so-good other things, it only brings us down. We need to draw the line on that type of boundary because nothing good comes from it. If we don't, we will end up being like this.

When people are positive, happy, nice, upbeat, and more, it brings out the best in others to be this way as well.

We all have bad days, and we are not always so positive and happy. I get that, and I understand this because I myself have these types of days. We are human, so not every day will go the way we want it to. That's when we have to practice on how to stay in peace, but that's another topic.

Like I said, it's okay to get like this now and then; but when someone is consistently like this, then it is time to cut the cord and focus back on your spiritual boundaries. This is why it is so important to keep practicing spiritual boundaries.

When we feel great about who we are, there is no stopping us at what we can do.

Chapter 12

SELF-LOVE

S elf-love is where it begins. If we don't learn to love ourselves, then how do we expect others to love us? We must learn what self-love is if we want a better selfless life. When we are able to love who we are, then that is when we will be able to give freely, love more, be happy, not be bitter, and so much more.

If we don't have self-love, then we will never think we are good enough. We will keep on doubting ourselves. We will keep believing we can't have successes, and that we will never succeed in our goals.

Self-love isn't the only thing that will prevent us from succeeding. If we have a negative attitude, that won't get us very far either. When we have a negative mindset before we even try something, then expect to fail.

God didn't put us on this earth for us to go on living life this way. He put us here for a purpose and a reason. We have our journeys to live out. We can't live out our life's journeys if we are full of negativity and don't have self-love.

When people tell us we can't do something or we will never succeed, those negative seeds that are planted in our heads will make us believe we can't do it. This is why having self-love is important; because if we had self-love, then we would be able to block out those negative voices.

Self-love is also important to living well. It influences the image of who we choose for our mate, the image we project at work, and how we cope with the problems in our life. It is so important to our well-being as well. With that, I want you to know how to bring more self-love into your life.

You see, I used to think I wasn't good enough. I thought everyone else was better than me. I didn't always have the confidence I have today. I thank God every day for giving me the confidence I need. It is because of him that I'm able to believe in myself. I'm where I am today because of God. I was able to get my book done through prayers and having faith. Faith and prayers will get you through anything.

There are many reasons why I chose to write this book. I pray that it will help others. God is working in me as I write it. He gives me the wisdom to write for sure.

Self-love isn't something you can buy in a department store, beauty store, in the makeup department, etc. to make us feel good in the long hall. I mean, all that does is buy us temporary happiness. It does not fulfill our well-being.

Self-love isn't reading something inspirational or being in a new relationship. It's not even about finding something to make us happy; because if we are truly happy, then we don't have to try to find things to make us happy.

Self-love is a state of appreciation for oneself that grows from actions that support our physical, psychological, and spiritual growth. Self-love is dynamic. It grows by actions that make us mature. When we act in ways that expand self-love in us, we begin to accept weaknesses much better as well as our strengths. We have fewer shortcomings. We have compassion for others and ourselves. We don't struggle to find personal meaning in things. Instead of doing that, we feel content within our soul. Our personal meaning in our life is centered around purpose, value, and wanting to do more for ourselves. Yes, this is what self-love is.

Loving ourselves should be one of the easiest things we can do. But some of us struggle with it. Some of us may struggle with self-love also because we feel we aren't as good as everybody else. We may even have resentment for someone else who we think is better looking than us. We may have resentment if someone has a better car, house, job, etc. By the way, material things don't bring us true happiness. When we have self-love, we don't feel this way.

I've mentioned this before, and I'll say it again. There's something I live by, and it is this: When we run our own race and not look at what others are doing, we get ahead faster in life. We are able to succeed in our goals. We are focused on our own accomplishments and not others. We are not focused on being in competition with others.

I don't think I'm the best hairstylist around, but I'm happy how far I've come in my career as a hairstylist. I don't look at what others are doing. I run my own race, and I can care less who owns their own salon. That doesn't matter to me. I can say I'm happy to see others do great in life and succeed. This makes me happy when I see this. I love seeing other hairstylists work. Do you know why I feel this way? It's because I have self-love.

In order to love ourselves, we must learn how to appreciate ourselves and what we have. Nobody is perfect, and nothing is perfect. Let's face it, we live in an imperfect world. Heck, I'm imperfect; and I love being imperfect. We all have flaws, make mistakes, and fall short.

Some people will say, "Oh, if I love myself, then it makes me sound conceited." Well I'm here to say, that is far from the truth, and nobody should ever feel this way. There is a big difference between someone who has self-love and someone who is conceited.

When someone is conceited, that person is stuck on themselves. This just means they think they are better than everybody else. They think they can do no wrong, and everyone else is wrong. They think they are smarter than the average person. They are always in competition with others. This is not self-love.

When we have self-love, we are down-to-earth, genuine, sweet, caring, etc. We put others before ourselves. We are selfless.

When we are or were in a bad relationship/marriage, self-love gets lost. If the person we are with makes us feel awful, brings us down, calls us bad names, doesn't give us compliments, and throws us down, our well-being suffers. They may even call us fat or say things like, "I'm surprised you want to eat because you are so fat. I'm not sure why I'm even with you." This is mental abuse, and nobody should ever have to go through this. Never think of yourself like this because it'll just bring you down. Get away from this type of behavior before it destroys you like a disease.

There are many reasons why people put us down. A few of the reasons for this are, they are not happy with themselves. They are insecure with themselves. They feel better about themselves when they are able to make others miserable. And some people are just plain miserable, so they want others to be miserable too.

Self-love in this behavior becomes lost because we start believing these lies that are told to us. Our minds are being brainwashed. It's a sad situation to be in. You feel awful about the person you are. You feel you are not good enough. God didn't design us to be in this situation. You can get help if you feel like you can't get past what others put into your head. Talking to a counselor will help. By the way, there is nothing wrong with talking to a counselor. It will actually benefit you, and you will feel better too.

You will have the strength to move forward no matter how bad people may have brainwashed you. When we look deep inside our souls and start loving who we are, that is when this too will pass. When you feel like you are not strong, think again because you are. Block out those negative voices you hear, and let in the positive voices. Think about all the good that's in your life. Think about how great you are and all the accomplishments you have made in your life. Look in the mirror daily and say, "I'm awesome, courageous, attractive, strong, smart, witty, and anything else that you can come up with to give yourself that ego you need. Hang around others who bring out the best in you.

Your relationship with yourself is arguably the most important one you'll ever have. At the beginning, throughout, and at the end of the day, it's always you. No matter how hard you try, you just cannot escape that voice in your head that can build you up or break you down. It can squash your dreams or push you to keep going.

Learning self-love is a process. It is one that takes time and commitment, but it is so worth it.

So now that we know what self-love is, we can now practice on how to always love ourselves. In the following paragraphs, I will list a seven-step guide on how to do just that.

Step 1: *Notice how you treat yourself.* Be mindful of the way you talk, how you talk about, and how you treat yourself. Listen and notice, "How am I talking to myself? How am I treating myself? What standards am I holding myself to?" Likely they are much higher than those you hold for others. That's okay because awareness is the first step to change.

Step 2: *Change your language.* Stop putting yourself down and minimizing your strengths or achievements. Our words are powerful, they create our reality. The more you declare something about yourself, the more you will feel and become it. You can easily reframe your words to be more positive and supportive. For example, replace "I am fat" or "I am a binge eater" with "my body is finding its rightful weight" or "I am learning how to nourish myself."

Step 3: *Have self-compassion.* Practice treating yourself as you would a friend or a child. When talking to yourself, think, *Is this something that I would say to my best friend?* If not, then change it to be more supportive and encouraging. Self-compassion releases self-hatred that keeps us stuck in our heads and beating ourselves up. This is one of the most critical steps to self-love. If you can't have compassion for yourself, it's going to be very difficult to take the next steps: forgiveness and acceptance.

Step 4: *Forgive yourself.* We all make mistakes—every single one of us. Just as you forgive your loved ones for their mistakes, you can also forgive yourself. Forgiveness is a powerful act of self-love. It allows us to release all the negative energy, thoughts, and rumination that simmers when we denounce ourselves.

Step 5: *Know yourself.* Take the time to objectively learn and understand who you really are, not who you think you should be. Explore all your strengths, weaknesses, and limits without judgment. Self-knowledge is key to being able to set boundaries and limits to respect and honor yourself. Choosing to honor yourself is one step closer to self-love.

Step 6: *Have self-acceptance.* Use self-compassion to start accepting all of you—the good, the bad, and the ugly—just as you do with your partner, friends, and family. Do you love every single thing about them? Probably not. But you accept them for all they are because no one is perfect, and there is no reason to hold yourself to a higher, impossible standard. Our level of self-acceptance determines our happiness. The more self-acceptance you have, the more happiness you will permit yourself to have.

Step 7: *Invest in yourself.* Make a commitment to invest the time for this. Start small, and be patient with yourself. You need to take each step to get there, but just five to ten minutes a day can be enough. Mindful practice will redirect and reframe your thoughts and inner critic to be kinder. Journaling (forgiveness and positive prompts) and gratitude exercises can help you release negative thoughts and refocus on all the things you appreciate and like about yourself.

The more you practice and focus on all the good about you, the easier these steps will be. Find a ritual that works best for you, and know that every little step is getting you closer to loving yourself.

Chapter 13

LIVING LIFE YOUR WAY

It's easy to get sidetracked in our life. We tend to listen to others and what they want for us. We tend to forget what it is that we want. We are so used to listening to others that we forget about what it is we need to do for ourselves and how we can make our lives better.

Your friends and family want what's best for you. But at the end of the day, it's you who matters. It's your life. It's your empire. It's what you want that matters. I'm not saying not to take advice and listen to it, but just make sure the choices you make are yours. If they aren't, then you will have regrets down the road.

If you continue to let people control your life, you will be miserable, and you'll have resentment as well.

Let's face it, the days and years are going by so fast. You don't want to be sixty and wonder where the heck your life has gone. You don't want to have regrets of not doing things you've always wanted to do but didn't.

I'm forty-five, and I'm wondering how the heck that happen. I feel like it went by in a blur. It's funny how when I was in my twenties, I thought forties and fifties were old but not anymore.

You have the choice on how you will live your life, but make sure you are always choosing the best and good choices. If you choose to go down the wrong path in life, keep in mind, there will be consequences.

As we get older, we tend to figure out what it is we want and don't want. Well most of us anyways.

When it comes to finding your mate, it is okay to be picky. In fact, you should be. You should never settle. Being alone isn't such a bad thing. It's better to be alone than being with someone who is not right for you. Life isn't long enough to be with someone because you don't want to be alone. Be with the person you are with for all the right reasons. Never sell yourself short or think you can't do better than someone you are currently with. Don't be with someone who mistreats you because you don't want to be alone.

I know the chapter of this is called "Living Life Your Way," but you don't have to live it alone. Take the advice from others; because when we are in a situation, we can't always see the whole picture clearly. Generally, others who are looking on the outside can see things a lot clearer. When we are away from the situation we were once in, we can see things clearer.

Sometimes we don't even realize we are settling. I mean, I didn't when I was with someone. Others could see it, but I didn't. Looking back now, I realized that I was settling.

I am with a great guy now, and I'm not settling. We've been together for three years. And as we know, nothing is perfect, but we try to make it as perfect as we can. It all comes down to trust, love, commitment, and communication. These are just a few ingredients we take to make a relationship work.

Sometimes when we live life our way, it's not always easy. It's not always easy making the right decisions or knowing if we made the right decisions. That's why it is important to seek advice if you feel you need to. Keep in mind, when you are in doubt of something or are questioning something that doesn't feel right, it generally means you already know the answer to your question.

Living life your way is the best thing you can do for yourself.

If you choose to go to college for something, make sure that it's your choice. Don't go for all the wrong reasons. If your parents want you to go to college for something you don't want to study, then you have to speak up; because if you don't, then you won't be happy. In order to live life your way, you must stand up for yourself. Your parents may get upset with your choice, but it's better for them to know what you really want to take up in college or if you even want to go to college.

As parents, they want what's best for their children. You may have heard your parents say, "Just wait until you have kids, then you'll know what it's like to be a parent." I'm sure there's truth to it. But when we were kids, we didn't see this. I won't know the feeling since I'm forty-five and won't be having kids. My boyfriend has five kids, so that's enough. I mean, I've always wanted kids, and I've been told that I would have made a great mom, but it wasn't in the cards for me. But I'm fine with it. I honestly love the life that God has given me.

When you are happy, secure, content, and more, it is easier to live life your way. It is easier to be in a relationship with someone as well. If we are just looking for someone to make us happy, it isn't going to work. You must be happy with yourself and find your own kind of happiness before you can even think of being in a relationship with another. If you don't, then you'll never be completely happy.

Life can be hard at times, but if we stay stuck in the situation we are in, life will only get harder. There is always a positive way out of a negative situation. God never promised us a rose garden, but what he did promise us is that he will be there for us every step of the way.

Living life our way can be a bit of a challenge at times. I certainly get it. When we are in doubt about something, then we need to seek God. When I have doubts about something, when I worry, or feel anxious, I turn to God. Give all your worries to God, and put it all in his hands. God is waiting on us to turn to him and give him our problems. We should be talking and praying to God daily. Believe me, it helps. When we are in a situation and feel like things won't get better, they will. They will get better because God is working behind the scenes in our life to make things better.

To make things clear, I turn to God in the not-so-good times as well as the good moments in my life. I thank him daily for all he has done for me and for all he will continue to do in my life.

This is what we should be doing. We should not just seek God in the bad times but also in the good times too.

Like I said, living life our way isn't always easy. That's why we need to ask God for guidance and direction. Allow him to lead the way. Allow him to lead you on the right path he has designed you to be on. Sometimes we get off the wrong path in life, but it is never too late to begin again, turn around, and head in the right direction. God gives us the freedom to make our own choices, so make sure you are making the right choices. He answers our prayers. They may not get answered right away, but all in good time, they will. One of my favorite quotes is that "unasked prayers go unanswered." That is so true. So while you are living life your way, ask God for help, and ask him to put you on the right path in your life's journey.

If I didn't change my life, it would never have changed on its own. What I mean by this is that I was working two jobs. I worked as a CNA and a hairdresser at the same time. I was miserable and stressed out. Money is great, but it doesn't bring you true happiness. I chose to take the leap of faith and quit my CNA job and made hairdressing my full-time career. I became a much happier person. I love being a hairstylist.

Think about how great you'll feel when you start living life your way. In the next paragraphs, I'm going to give you some advice on how to live life your way and how to be happy in the same process.

1. *Write your own story.* Once you have envisioned the life you really want for yourself, start taking small steps to actually live your dream life. Whenever you're about to make a decision—no matter how small—look at your own life story, the one you have written on your own, and ask yourself, "Is this decision going to take me closer to my dream life?" You need a strong will. You can always dream of an ideal life, but you can only get there with a commitment on your side to get closer to it every single day.

2. *Follow your dreams.* If there are things you're really good at, you really love with all your heart, and you're truly interested in, pursue it with perseverance. It is not a coincidence that the word passion was derived from a Latin word that means "to suffer." Passion is overrated. The real question is,

what do you want to do with the thing you're so passionate about? Do you want to keep working on it? Do you want to be better at it? Do you want to master it? Do you want to do something good with it? Do you want to share it with those who need it? How much you're willing to suffer for your passion is what separates movers from dreamers.

3. *Give (and be) your best, always.* Make sure that you do your very best in every single thing that you do, no matter what it is. Brewing a cup of coffee, preparing a simple lunch, getting caught in a terrible traffic jam, mopping the floor, hugging a friend, holding your lover's hands—whatever you do, always strive to do your best. Give your best at that very moment. Always ask yourself, "How can I give more? How can I make people happier or feel better after they interact with me? How can I offer more of myself, my skills, my talents, or anything else that I have to the people around me?

4. *Deliver the unexpected.* When someone asks you for a cup of coffee, give him a cup of coffee and a slice of banana cake on the side with a personalized thank-you note. Give them more. Give them more of you, and give more to yourself too. Try doing this in every aspect of your life, and you'll see how it will change you from the inside.

5. *Just go ahead.* As a struggling perfectionist, when it comes to my passion-driven projects, I find solace in reading and watching a good movie. If you want to write a novel, write one page a day, and in a year, you will have a 365-page novel. If you want to have a food photography exhibition, start by taking a picture of a person's breakfast every single day, and in a year, you'll have a collection of 365 breakfast meals of 365 people. Just do something now. Don't wait for something to be perfect because it will never be. Don't wait until you get better at something because you will always want to be better than better. Don't wait until something happens because you won't have any guarantee that it will happen. Stop making excuses. Just go ahead.

6. *Step out of your comfort zone.* Do the things you won't normally do. Change the ordinary. Face your fear. Do not settle for less. The more it feels challenging or frightening, the more reason you need to do it because it means that you're about to cross a junction in your life that will take you further in life.

The idea here is not to be successful in it. If you're afraid of riding a roller coaster, you are allowed to ride on it while closing your eyes and screaming your heart out and crying excessively afterward. It is okay. What's important is to know that you have tried. You just need to remind yourself, again and again, how resilient you are to know that no matter what life throws out at you, you'll be ready to face it because you know everything will be okay, that you will always survive.

It's just like those times when you dare yourself to fall in love again and find your heart broken again, but you end up smiling after a while, knowing that it only makes you stronger because you know that you have the capacity to love someone so much and that you will always have the courage to try again. The same goes for loving life.

So many of us have a tendency to hesitate when faced with a difficult task or decision. While it's definitely important to analyze situations carefully before taking any drastic measures, you don't want to be so fearful that you don't make a move at all. Remove any doubts you might have about your abilities. Be confident in your capacity to weather any storm that comes your way. You've made it this far, haven't you?

In order to succeed, you need to take a look at the first stair in front of you rather than looking at the full staircase. If you don't do this, then fear will hold you back. This is all part of living your life in a more stress-free zone.

Start living your life for yourself. No matter what others say and do, no matter what society is doing, if it's not for you, then don't do it. If you don't believe something is for you, if it doesn't make your heart sing a happy tune, then don't do it. Go your own way, and build a life beyond your wildest dreams. Keep striving to the top because you got this. Furthermore, never give up on yourself and being the best you can possibly be.

Chapter 14

ANXIETY AND DEPRESSION

I know this is not the most inspiring topic to talk about, but I feel that people need to know what anxiety and depression are as they go on living their life's journey. Not everyone is aware of the symptoms that come with anxiety and depression. I, for starters, certainly did not know all the signs and symptoms that came with anxiety. I just found out three years ago the symptoms I had that stemmed from anxiety. I've had these symptoms pretty much all my life and didn't even know it. Looking back now, I noticed my anxiety progress when I was in my twenties.

Anxiety and depression are real. They do not go away by putting a Band-Aid on them like you would a cut. We wish it could be that simple. People don't choose to be depressed or to have anxiety issues.

A chemical imbalance in the brain is said to occur when the brain has either excessive or insufficient chemicals called neurotransmitters. Neurotransmitters are natural chemicals that help ease the communication between your nerve cells. Examples include norepinephrine and serotonin. Having insufficient levels of these neurotransmitters may cause anxiety and depression. It's often said that mental health conditions, such as depression and anxiety, are caused by a chemical imbalance in the brain. Conditions can be caused by an imbalance of neurotransmitters between nerve cells in the brain. The exact cause of mental health conditions is still unclear. Researchers believe that genetics, as well as environmental and social factors, such as stress or trauma, play a role. Scientists in the late 1950s proposed the idea that mental health conditions are caused by chemical imbalance of the brain.

These researchers hypothesized that insufficient levels of neurotransmitters can lead to symptoms such as:

- feelings of sadness, helplessness, worthlessness, or emptiness
- overeating or a loss of appetite
- insomnia or sleeping too much
- restlessness
- irritability
- a feeling of impending doom or danger
- a lack of energy
- distancing yourself from others
- a feeling of numbness or a lack of empathy
- extreme changes in mood
- thoughts of hurting yourself or others
- difficulty carrying out day-to-day activities
- a feeling of hearing voices in your head
- alcohol or drug misuse
- difficulty concentrating

It's unfortunate that it happens, but it is not your fault that you have it. Some people may think that if you train your thoughts, then that will cure it. Or people might say, "Well, if people had more faith, then it'll go away." As nice as that sounds, unfortunately, all this has nothing to do with that at all. We can't just shut our brain off or pretend that there is nothing wrong. However, there is hope for both anxiety and depression. Later, I'll be talking more about it.

Losing a loved one when one passes on, getting fired from a job, going through a divorce, and going through other difficult situations can lead a person to be sad, lonely, and scared. Even though these feelings are normal reactions to life's heartaches, they could easily turn into depression. That's why it doesn't hurt to talk to a counselor. That's why God gave these people the talents they need for people who need someone to help them sort out their feelings and for them to help these people out.

Most people go through periods of not being happy or being sad at times, but then it passes. This is normal. But what is not normal is someone not wanting to get out of bed, someone who doesn't want to go to work at all, or someone who doesn't desire to do anything. They don't even want to go for walks, meet up with friends, or watch TV. This is severe depression. The person is diagnosed with a psychiatric disorder (relating to mental illness or its treatment). Low moods are much severe, and they tend to persist.

Depression occurs more often in women than men. In men, it manifests often as tiredness, irritability, and anger. They may show more reckless behavior or abuse drugs and alcohol. They also tend to not recognize that they are depressed and fail to seek help.

In women, depression tends to manifest as sadness, worthlessness, and guilt.

In younger children, depression is more likely to manifest as school refusal or anxiety when separated from their parent(s). They worry about their loved one dying.

Depressed teenagers tend to be irritable, sulky, and get into trouble, whether in or outside of school. They may also have frequent comorbid anxiety, eating disorders, or substance abuse. Older adults' depression may manifest more subtly as they tend to be less likely to admit to feelings of sadness, grief, and medical illnesses. This is more common in our population.

As you can see, depression affects adults, younger children, teenagers, men, and women differently. Keep in mind that some of the same depression symptoms can happen in teenagers, men, women, and adults.

There is definitely a difference when it comes to depression and anxiety. Many people struggle to know what the difference is between the two of them. This is because many people with anxiety also develop depression and vice versa. Some don't even know they have anxiety or depression. But not to get confused, just because someone has anxiety doesn't mean they'll get depression and vice versa. For example, I don't have depression, but I have anxiety.

Nearly 50 percent of people diagnosed with depression will also be diagnosed with anxiety disorder. However, it is important to accurately diagnose the problem in order to treat the condition.

Many people with depression may experience what is known as anxious distress. In addition to their low mood, people with anxious distress often feel tense, restless, and have trouble concentrating. They have trouble concentrating because they worry so much. They are deeply afraid that something bad is going to happen to them or to someone else. They may also worry that they may lose control of themselves. People who experience anxious distress with depression may be at a higher risk of suicide or need more intense treatment. It is so important to identify these symptoms along with depression.

It's important to let your doctor or mental health professional elevate you to see if your symptoms meet the criteria for a depressive disorder or an anxiety disorder.

Symptoms of major depression are the following:

- Depressed mood
- Lack of interest in enjoyable activities
- Increase or decrease in appetite
- Insomnia or hypersomnia
- Slowing of movement
- Lack of energy
- Feelings of guilt or worthlessness
- Trouble concentrating
- Suicidal thoughts or behavior

For a diagnosis of major depressive disorder, a person needs to have experienced five or more of these symptoms for at least two weeks.

People experiencing some of these symptoms might also be diagnosed with persistent depressive disorder (also called dysthymia), premenstrual dysphoric disorder, or a depressive disorder due to another condition. They may meet the criteria for bipolar disorder if they also experience symptoms of mania.

Persistent depressive disorder is a mild but long-term form of depression. Dysthymia is defined as a low mood occurring for at least two years, along with at least two other symptoms of depression.

Premenstrual dysphoric disorder (PMDD) is a severe, sometimes disabling extension of premenstrual syndrome (PMS). Although PMS and PMDD both have physical and emotional symptoms, PMDD causes extreme mood shifts that can disrupt daily life and damage relationships.

In both PMDD and PMS, symptoms usually begin seven to ten days before your period starts and continue for the first few days of your period.

Both PMDD and PMS may cause bloating, breast tenderness, fatigue, and changes in sleep and eating habits. In PMDD, however, at least one of these emotional and behavioral symptoms stands out:

- Sadness or hopelessness
- Anxiety or tension
- Extreme moodiness
- Marked irritability or anger

The cause of PMDD isn't clear. Underlying depression and anxiety are common in both PMS and PMDD, so it's possible that the hormonal changes that trigger a menstrual period worsen the symptoms of mood disorders.

Treatment of PMDD is directed at preventing or minimizing symptoms and may include the following:

- *Antidepressants.* Selective serotonin reuptake inhibitors (SSRIs), such as fluoxetine (Prozac, Sarafem, and others) and sertraline (Zoloft), may reduce emotional symptoms, fatigue, food cravings, and sleep problems. You can reduce symptoms of PMDD by taking SSRIs all month or only during the interval between ovulation and the start of your period.

- *Birth control pills.* Taking birth control pills with no pill-free interval or with a shortened pill-free interval may reduce PMS and PMDD symptoms.
- *Nutritional supplements.* Consuming 1,200 milligrams of calcium daily may possibly reduce symptoms of PMS and PMDD. Vitamin B$_6$, magnesium, and L-tryptophan may also help, but talk with your doctor for advice before taking any supplements.
- *Herbal remedies.* Some research suggests that chasteberry (Vitex agnus-castus) may possibly reduce irritability, mood swings, breast tenderness, swelling, cramps, and food cravings associated with PMDD, but more research is needed. The US Food and Drug Administration doesn't regulate herbal supplements, so talk with your doctor before trying one.
- *Diet and lifestyle changes.* Regular exercise often reduces premenstrual symptoms. Cutting back on caffeine, avoiding alcohol, and stopping smoking may ease symptoms too. Getting enough sleep and using relaxation techniques, such as mindfulness, meditation, and yoga, may also help. Avoid stressful and emotional triggers, such as arguments over financial issues or relationship problems, whenever possible.

If you have symptoms of PMDD, talk with your doctor about testing and treatment option.

Major depressive disorder or clinical depression affects how you feel, think, and behave and can lead to a variety of emotional and physical problems. You may have trouble doing normal day-to-day activities, and sometimes you may feel as if life isn't worth living.

More than just a bout of the blues, depression isn't a weakness, and you can't simply "snap out" of it. Depression may require long-term treatment. But don't get discouraged. Most people with depression feel better with medication, psychotherapy, or both.

Although depression may occur only once during your life, people typically have multiple episodes. During these episodes, symptoms occur most of the day, nearly every day and may include the following:

- Feelings of sadness, tearfulness, emptiness, or hopelessness
- Angry outbursts, irritability, or frustration even over small matters
- Loss of interest or pleasure in most or all normal activities, such as sex, hobbies, or sports
- Sleep disturbances, including insomnia, or sleeping too much
- Tiredness and lack of energy—so even small tasks take extra effort
- Reduced appetite and weight loss or increased cravings for food and weight gain
- Anxiety, agitation, or restlessness
- Slowed thinking, speaking, or body movements
- Feelings of worthlessness or guilt, fixating on past failures or self-blame
- Trouble thinking, concentrating, making decisions, and remembering things
- Frequent or recurrent thoughts of death, suicidal thoughts, suicide attempts, or suicide
- Unexplained physical problems, such as back pain or headaches

For many people with depression, symptoms usually are severe enough to cause noticeable problems in day-to-day activities, such as work, school, social activities, or relationships with others. Some people may feel generally miserable or unhappy without really knowing why.

What is PMS? Premenstrual syndrome (PMS) is a monthly pattern of symptoms that start about a week before your period. These symptoms tend to go away within four days after starting your period.

For many people, PMS causes both physical and psychological symptoms, including the following:

- bloating
- digestive issues
- headaches
- breast tenderness
- mood swings
- irritability
- anxiety
- insomnia
- confusion
- depressed mood

The severity of these symptoms varies from person to person. Some people also experience a more severe form of PMS called premenstrual dysphoric disorder (PMDD). People with PMDD experience at least five of these symptoms. The symptoms are often incredibly intense and get in the way of day-to-day activities.

Experts aren't sure about the exact causes of PMS or PMDD, although they're likely related to changes in your levels of estrogen and progesterone, two hormones that play a big role in your menstrual cycle. There may also be other factors involved.

Oral contraceptives and antidepressants are traditional treatments for PMS and PMDD. There are also several supplements you may want to try for relief, often with fewer side effects than traditional treatments.

Here are some natural supplements for PMS and how to use them safely:

1. Chasteberry

    Chasteberry is one of the most commonly used supplements for female reproductive health. A 2013 review of its benefits for the female reproductive system suggests it provides many benefits for people with PMS.

It was shown to be particularly helpful for physical symptoms, including bloating, breast pain, and headaches. It even appeared to work better than fluoxetine (Prozac), an antidepressant, for these symptoms. However, it was less effective than fluoxetine at treating psychological symptoms, like mood swings, in people with PMDD.

How to take it: Always follow the manufacturer's dosage guidelines.

Safety: Talk to your doctor before taking chasteberry if you have a hormone-sensitive condition, such as ER-positive breast cancer. Chasteberry may also interact with oral contraceptives and antipsychotic medications. You should speak with your doctor first if you take any of these drugs.

2. Calcium

People with PMS symptoms often don't get enough calcium from their diet. Calcium levels may also change throughout your menstrual cycle.

A 2017 clinical trial from a trusted source found that calcium supplements helped to reduce some symptoms of PMS, like bloating and fatigue. More so, they concluded that calcium supplementation was effective for reducing psychological symptoms, including sadness, mood swings, and anxiety.

You don't have to start with a pill if you're looking to up your calcium levels. Start by adding some calcium-rich foods to your diet. If that isn't doing it, calcium supplements are available.

How to take it: Start by taking 500 milligrams (mg) per day. It's good to keep in mind that the daily recommended allowance for calcium in adults ranges from 1,000 to 1,300 mg, depending on your age and sex.

Safety: Calcium supplements are safe for most people, but they may cause constipation in higher doses. Talk to your doctor if you take any other medications, including thyroid hormones or antibiotics. You may need to take them at different times of the day. You should also not take supplements if you've had kidney stones or other health issues. Talk to your doctor if you're unsure.

3. Vitamin B_6

    Vitamin B_6 is involved in the production of neurotransmitters, which play a big role in your moods. Vitamin B_6 is a water-soluble vitamin found in many foods you eat, including the following:

    - chickpeas
    - tuna, salmon, and other fish
    - potatoes and other starchy veggies
    - beef liver and organ meat

    Several small studies have found that taking a daily vitamin B_6 supplement may help with many of the psychological symptoms of PMS, including moodiness, irritability, and anxiety. However, conclusions are still limited due to poor quality of the current research.

    How to take it: Daily intake of water-soluble vitamins is needed because the body doesn't store B_6. If you can't get enough from your diet, supplement with 50 to 100 mg per day. Always follow the manufacturer's dosage guidelines.

    Safety: Don't take vitamin B_6 supplements if you take cycloserine, anti-seizure medications, or theophylline.

4. Magnesium

    Some women with PMS may have low levels of magnesium. With this in mind, a 2010 study from a trusted source found that supplementing with a combination of magnesium and vitamin B_6 helped participant's ease their PMS symptoms, including depression, anxiety, insomnia, water retention, and breast tenderness.

    Foods high in magnesium include the following:

    - almonds
    - green leafy vegetables
    - peanuts

If you want to try the combination used in the study, you can buy supplements that combine magnesium and vitamin B_6 in a single tablet.

How to take it: Take 200 to 250 mg per day, keeping in mind that the average daily recommendation for adults should be around 300–400 mg (as per a trusted source), depending on age and sex. Always follow the manufacturer's dosage guidelines.

Safety: Talk to your doctor before taking a magnesium supplement if you also take proton pump inhibitors, diuretics, antibiotics, or bisphosphonates. If you take any of these, you may still be able to take magnesium supplements, but you'll likely need to take them at different times of day.

5. Essential fatty acids

Certain fatty acids, such as gamma-linoleic acid and alpha-linoleic acid, have anti-inflammatory effects that may help with PMS symptoms. Gamma linoleic acid is found in evening primrose oil, which has a long history of being used for PMS. However, more research is needed to back up its uses for PMS symptoms.

Still a 2011 study from a trusted source found that a mixture of essential fatty acids that included gamma linoleic acid, oleic acid, and linoleic acid reduced PMS symptoms in people who took 1 to 2 grams of the mixture every day. This improvement in symptoms was stronger after six months of taking the oil mixture compared to results after three months. You can buy supplements containing a similar blend of essential fatty acids.

How to use: Follow the manufacturer's dosage guidelines for the blend you choose.

Safety: Talk to your doctor before taking an essential fatty acid supplement if you take any other medications or herbal supplements. This is especially important if you take an anticoagulant or antipsychotic medications.

6. Ginkgo biloba

    Ginkgo biloba is best known as an herbal remedy for improving memory, but it can also help with PMS symptoms.

    A clinical study in 2009 evaluated its use for treating PMS symptoms. Researchers found that taking 40 mg tablets three times per day reduced the severity of both physical and psychological symptoms in the students studied.

    How to use: Follow the manufacturer's instructions for dosage. Start with the lowest recommended dose and take for about ten to fourteen days from midcycle until a day or two after your period.

    Safety: This herb can have serious interactions with medications you're taking. Talk to your doctor if you have any questions or concerns. Don't take ginkgo biloba if you've ever had a seizure. You should also talk to your doctor before taking a ginkgo biloba supplement if you also take blood thinners, such as aspirin or warfarin, or have diabetes.

7. St. John's wort

    Many consider St. John's wort to be an herbal alternative to prescription antidepressants. It affects both serotonin and norepinephrine, two neurotransmitters that affect your mood and that are typically targeted in traditional antidepressants.

    Although St. John's wort is better known for treating depression, it's one of the most thoroughly studied medicinal herbs, with several studies pointing to its effectiveness in treating PMS symptoms. For example, a 2010 study from a trusted source found that it improved both physical and emotional symptoms, particularly depression and anxiety.

    How to use: Dosage recommendations vary significantly depending on the manufacturer. You should follow their recommendations, but it's advised not to take this herb longer than six weeks.

Safety: St. John's wort is a powerful herb that can interact with many types of medication, including antidepressants, commonly used to treat PMS. This herb can also interfere with birth control and heart and blood pressure medications. Talk to your doctor before taking St. John's wort if you take any type of medication, including other supplements. When taking St. John's wort, make sure to apply sunscreen before going outside as this supplement can make your skin more sensitive to sunlight.

The bottom line is that for many people, PMS is a frustrating monthly ordeal. However, there are several supplements that may help with both your physical and emotional symptoms.

Many supplements actually become more effective over time, so don't be disappointed if you don't notice immediate results. Some may take three to six months to work.

But remember, natural remedies—although natural—aren't necessarily harmless. Always check with your doctor first if you take any other medication or have an underlying condition of any kind.

The next topic I'll be talking about is generalized anxiety. Generalized anxiety makes you overthink things. It makes you question things. It puts ideas in your head that have not even taken place. It makes you second guess your decision-making and causes you to have trust issues. It also makes you feel insecure, worry without end, takes over your life, and it makes you feel like you are alone.

I have this type of anxiety. Although I've learned not to say "my anxiety" because it is not my anxiety. I don't own it, and God certainly didn't give it to me.

I found out three years ago that I had it. Like I had mentioned before, I always had this anxiety but never quite knew all these symptoms that came with it. I just thought anxiety consists of getting nervous and being anxious a little bit. I didn't know it was more than that. I'm not going to lie, it is an awful thing to have to go through. It is real, and it takes over your life. I found it hard being in a relationship because of it. Some people will say, "Oh, just think positive, and it will get better," or "stop being anxious." It's not that easy to be able to shut off what your brain is saying, nor is it easy to just relax. I wish it were that easy. I'll tell you, what works is praying. I prayed to God and said I was tired of living my life in fear, anxiety, insecurity, and so forth. My prayers were answered. I'm not saying I don't have bad moments and days anymore, but it is nothing like it was.

I was working at Shady Knoll at the time when I had a bad anxiety attack. I felt like I was going to have a nervous breakdown. I was like, "Okay, it is time to call the doctor." I felt like God led me to get the help I needed. I was taking Lexapro, but it only worked for a year. Now I'm on Trintellix. I've been on that for two years now, and for the most part, it works.

By the way, Shady Knoll is a nursing home, and I went in and did the residents' hair there. I worked there from December of 2016 until November of 2019.

Some of the symptoms that come with generalized anxiety are the following:

- Excessive worry
- Restlessness
- Being easily fatigued
- Trouble concentrating
- Irritability
- Sleep disturbance
- Muscle tension
- Having trust issues
- Insecurity issues

If you experience any of these symptoms most days, and they are causing you distress in your daily life, then consider going to a doctor or a counselor. God doesn't want us living life this way. He wants us all to be happy.

There is a really great place called the Wellness Center located in Oxford, Connecticut. I heard really great things about them. I have a few friends who go there as well. Like I said, there is nothing wrong with talking to a counselor.

It might help as well if we reprogram our thoughts. It's like reprogramming a computer. Sometimes, if we have to shift our brain to think differently and be more positive, that might help.

Others types of anxiety disorders are obsessive-compulsive disorder known as OCD, panic disorder, social phobia, and post-traumatic stress disorder known as PTSD

Obsessive-compulsive disorder is an anxiety disorder and is characterized by recurrent, unwanted thoughts (obsessions) and/or repetitive behaviors (compulsions). Repetitive behaviors, such as hand washing, counting, checking, or cleaning are often performed with the hope of preventing obsessive thoughts or making them go away. Performing these so-called "rituals," however, provides only temporary relief, and not performing them markedly increases anxiety.

Panic disorder is an anxiety disorder and is characterized by unexpected and repeated episodes of intense fear, accompanied by physical symptoms that may include chest pain, heart palpitations, shortness of breath, dizziness, or abdominal distress.

Social phobia or social anxiety disorder is an anxiety disorder characterized by overwhelming anxiety and excessive self-consciousness in everyday social situations. Social phobia can be limited to only one type of situation, such as a fear of speaking in formal or informal situations, eating or drinking in front of others, or, in its most severe form, may be so broad that a person experiences symptoms almost anytime they are around other people.

Post-traumatic stress disorder (PTSD) is an anxiety disorder that can develop after exposure to a terrifying event or ordeal in which grave physical harm occurred or was threatened. Traumatic events that may trigger PTSD include violent personal assaults, natural or human-caused disasters, accidents, or military combat.

While I'm sure there are more that come with anxiety disorder, these are said to be the main ones. Although there is another anxiety disorder that I would like to talk about, and that's separation anxiety, it is something that I've experienced. Like I said, these topics are not the most inspiring topics, but it's all about learning about them through your life's journey. You may not be going through this, but you may know someone who is, and you'll have some kind of education on how you can help another.

Separation anxiety is a normal stage of development for infants and toddlers. Young children often experience a period of separation anxiety, but most children outgrow separation anxiety by about three years of age. In some children, separation anxiety is a sign of a more serious condition known as separation anxiety disorder, starting as early as preschool age. If your child's separation anxiety seems intense or prolonged especially if it interferes with school or other daily activities or includes panic attacks or other problems, he or she may have separation anxiety disorder. Most frequently, this relates to the child's anxiety about his or her parents, but it could relate to another close caregiver. Less often, separation anxiety disorder can also occur in teenagers and adults, causing significant problems leaving home or going to work. But treatment can help.

Separation anxiety disorder is diagnosed when symptoms are excessive for the developmental age and cause significant distress in daily functioning.

Symptoms may include the following:

- Recurrent and excessive distress about anticipating or being away from home or loved ones
- Constant excessive worry about losing a parent or other loved one to an illness or a disaster
- Constant worry that something bad will happen, such as being lost or kidnapped, causing separation from parents or other loved ones
- Refusing to be away from home because of fear of separation
- Not wanting to be home alone and without a parent or other loved one in the house
- Reluctance or refusing to sleep away from home without a parent or other loved one nearby
- Repeated nightmares about separation
- Frequent complaints of headaches, stomachaches, or other symptoms when separation from a parent or other loved one is anticipated

Separation anxiety disorder may be associated with panic disorder and panic attacks, repeated episodes of sudden feelings of intense anxiety, and fear or terror that reach a peak within minutes.

When to see a doctor: Separation anxiety disorder usually won't go away without treatment and can lead to panic disorder and other anxiety disorders into adulthood. If you have concerns about your child's separation anxiety, talk to your child's pediatrician or other health care provider.

Sometimes, separation anxiety disorder can be triggered by life stress that results in separation from a loved one. Genetics may also play a role in developing the disorder. A death of a loved one may also cause this as well.

I've gone through separation anxiety when I was going out with someone. I would get bad separation anxiety if I didn't hear from him within a few hours at a time. This is an awful feeling and makes you feel like you are a crazy person. Even though I knew I wasn't, that's how it makes you feel. How I got through it was a lot of praying. But the medication I'm on helps with this too.

Having someone in your life helps make things better as well. Keep in mind, the person you are with should reassure you how much they love and mean to you and vice versa. I don't mean your partner has to reassure you every single minute but every now and then. It will make a world of difference.

Taking a look back on depression and anxiety, there is some similarity. We can see with both that there are sleep problems, trouble concentrating, fatigue, irritability, and lack of motivation.

There is a light at the end of the tunnel though. There is help for this. Go talk to your doctor or therapist, they'll help get you going in the right direction. It may be hard finding the best medication at first for your condition, but don't give up. You may have to try different medications to see what works best for you and your condition. Your doctor will find what will work for you and your condition.

The best thing you can do for yourself as well is to keep a little journal about how you are feeling, why or what made you get anxious or depressed. Try shifting your mind to think differently. Like I said, if we reprogram our thoughts, this might help. It's like reprogramming a computer. Sometimes, if we have to shift our brain to think differently and to be more positive, like anything, the more we do it, the easier it will come; and we will become better at it too. Write in a journal about your day-to-day activities. Write about how your day was too. Do this each day.

I'm not saying it'll cure what's going on, but it doesn't hurt to try, right? It may help diagnose what's going on with you too. Hey, I have a journal too, and I love it. It helps. Like I tell my friends, I would never give advice if it is not something that didn't work for me and something I wouldn't do.

Chapter 15

TIME MANAGEMENT

Time management is something I've always struggled with and still kinda do today.

I have a tendency to get sidetracked. Sometimes I jump from one thing to another. Some would think I have ADHD, but I don't. I'm just being a little sarcastic. I just have a little hard time organizing my time wisely. I hope, by writing this chapter, my time management skills will get better.

If you are like me, you probably feel like you need to be more organized and productive. Do you spend your day in a frenzy of activity and then wonder why you haven't accomplished much? Well then, I have great positive news for you! There are some awesome tips that will help you increase your time management skills and productivity. Get ready to stay cool, calm, and collective.

1. *Realize that time management is a myth.* This is the first thing we have to understand about time management. No matter how organized we are, there are only twenty-four hours in a day. Time doesn't change. All we can actually manage is ourselves and what we do with the time we have. Time slips away, so we have to make sure our time isn't being wasted on things that don't matter. Don't consume all of your time with being on your phone or by being on

social media. I know at times it's hard, but we must try and limit our time on it.

2. *Find out where you are wasting your time.* Many of us are familiar with time wasters.

You know the time we could be putting to good use but don't. We have to figure out what takes our time away from us doing things that we have to do. Figuring this out is key to better time management. Do you spend too much time net surfing, reading emails, posting and being on Facebook, texting, or making personal phone calls? If you are, then try limiting your time. A way you can do this is by setting an alarm to see how long your time is being taken up. Setting an alarm will help you stay on schedule, and it will allow you to get other things done as well.

3. *Create time management goals.* Remember, the focus of time management is actually changing your behaviors, not changing time. A good place to start is by eliminating your personal time wasters. For one week, set a goal that you're not going to take personal phone calls or respond to non-work-related text messages while you are working. Don't go on social media either. A good way to do this is to block out time on your schedule. Have a schedule you follow daily, and I'm sure this will help keep your time in check. It will also help organize your time more so you won't feel so overwhelmed with things. After a week, see how it goes. Save phone calls and text messages for lunchtime, or set aside a time at night to answer calls. Another good way is to write down things that you have to do the night before.

4. *Know the time management tools to use.* Whether it's a day timer, a software program, or a phone app, the first step to physically managing your time is to know where your time is being used. So if you put in the things you want to do for that day, you will easily be able to keep track of how much you are getting done. Putting things that you have to do on the calendar on your phone will help as well. You can also set daily reminders of what you have to do on your phone.

5.   Like I said, in order to have good prioritizing, organization, and time management skills, write down the night before a list of things you have to get done. Set reminders on your phone, limit your time on social media and being on your phone by setting an alarm to get off of it. Set an alarm for twenty minutes.

Go to bed at a reasonable time so you are not waking up late. Let's face it, when we don't wake up on time for work, we are rush to get out of the house. Make time to have breakfast in the morning. After all, that's the most important meal of the day. For instance, if you have to be at work at 9:00 a.m., then get up at 6:00 a.m. This way, you can have a chance to get ready, have breakfast, listen or read something inspirational, and maybe some time to do some exercise too. When we wake up in the morning and have a good mindset, it sets the tone for the day off to a good one.

Your time belongs to you. The most important time management tip of all is that you are in control. You are the only one who can make it all happen, well—and of course—with God's help as well. Pray, take a deep breath, and it'll all fall into place.

Chapter 16

INSPIRING QUOTES AND DEVOTIONALS

Well, this concludes my book, and what better way to conclude it by filling the last chapter with inspiring quotes.

1. At this very moment, God is working behind the scenes in your life to make things better. He is rearranging things in your favor. Stay in faith, never give up, and never stop believing.

2. And out of nowhere, God brings someone special in our lives. The best things happen unexpectedly. They happen in a blink of an eye. You know when something is meant to be because it comes naturally. It's not forced, and it isn't stressful.

3. We can't look for someone or things to make us happy. Happiness begins with us.

4. God loves us all and wants us to be happy.

5. I thank God all the time for all he has done in my life and all he will continue to do.

6. Whatever your beliefs are, never stop believing in yourself.

7. Never give up because you just never know what life will bring you.

8. I used to say, believe in yourself and anything is possible. But now I say, believe in yourself and God, and nothing is impossible.

9. Prayer is a powerful tool that not even the enemy can master.

10. We all have our purpose in this journey called life. Make yours count.

11. We all have talents. If we don't use them, then what good is it? It's like buying a car or something else and not using it.

12. You may have had some tough times in your life that you feel like giving up, but don't. It is never too late to start over and to make your life better than ever.

13. We all make mistakes. Let today be your day that you say, "I'm worthy, so I'm going to make my life better than ever."

14. Walk in faith, not by sight.

15. When you are tempted to get discouraged, remind yourself that according to God's word, your future looks spotless.

16. Don't think about the future nor the past, and just live for today.

17. You may not be where you want to be in your life, but you are not where you used to be either.

18. People may not always believe in you, and that's okay. They might try to crush your dreams. Push through the negativity. When they see you succeeded, they'll ask you how you got there.

19. You don't have to prove to anyone that you can do something. The only person you have to prove anything to is yourself.

20. Your life doesn't change until you change it.

21. The road to success doesn't happen on its own. It takes determination, commitment, and a strong will to succeed.

22. You are your own road to success and happiness. Believe in yourself, and you will be happy and will succeed.

23. Everyone needs some sort of encouragement. Try to show some love and encouragement for someone else that may need it.

24. Kindness is free, so give it. Caring is free, so show it. Love is free, so spread it around.

25. Don't judge a book by its cover. Don't judge someone you don't know because that person you just judged could be the nicest person ever.

26. Relationship tips: Be open, be honest, be you, be kind, be supportive, be respectful, be understanding, be loyal, know boundaries, give one another space and encouragement. Relationships/marriages are about giving your all 100 percent and not 50 percent.

27. Embrace the beauty of all of life's treasures.

28. Let love in, and let hatred leave your soul.

29. Don't search for love. Let love find you.

30. God is my light to the truth of all evil. He shields me from pain so I can gain the strength to be positive for a better tomorrow.

31. When others aren't being so nice to you, always know, you aren't what others say you are. Always find the good in yourself so when this does happen, you always feel good about who you are. Remember, opinions don't matter. You matter, so always believe in you.

32. When your one and only comes into your life, you'll just know. There will be no second-guessing, no game playing. It'll be an open, honest, true, real, and more of a relationship. It'll feel right. You'll just know you are meant to be. You'll see it in the eyes because the eyes don't lie.

33. And that moment is where it all makes sense. You begin to see the truth. You begin to break free. You begin again because you are worth more than the lies you were fed. Your ending is your new beginning.

34. It's not about finding the perfect person. It's about finding the perfect person who is right for you.

35. Don't judge someone because you refused to see the beauty inside of them.

36. The best things stem from the bottom up and blossom into something beautiful.

37. Yesterday is a memory, today is a given, and tomorrow will be a blessing to start a new day.

38. Yesterday is the past, today is the present, and tomorrow hasn't even been thought of.

39. Live in the now, and don't worry about the future nor the past.

40. Being a hairstylist is more than knowing how to do hair. It's about touching the lives of many. It's true that love is in the hair. But really, the beauty of it all comes from within.

41. Faith conquers all our fears, all of our anxieties, and every bad thing we are feeling inside our souls. Faith is what gets us through even when we feel like giving up.

42. Faith is where it is at. Faith is where it begins. And when we have faith, it is never-ending.

43. When life throws us bricks, get back up. Your life's journey isn't over. Just because you come across a few rough patches, it doesn't mean a thing. Turn the page because you still have more chapters in your life to live and tell about.

44. When one dream dies, another begins.

45. You may have had a bad day, but there really are no bad days. There's something good in the not-so-good days.

46. There certainly are times in all of our lives when bad things happen or things don't always turn out as we had hoped. That's when we must make a decision that we are going to be happy in spite of our circumstances.

47. Live life to the fullest with no regrets.

48. Your life is what you make it.

49. Do things now, otherwise, you will have regrets you didn't.

50. Live for today, and don't worry about tomorrow.

51. Design your life the way you want it, and embrace the beauty of it all.

52. Setbacks are sometimes a set up for something better.

53. Live life your way and not like another.

54. Run your own race. Don't look at what others are doing. If you do, then you won't succeed. Be your own inspiration and your biggest competitor.

55. Don't be a copycat of someone else.
56. It's not about how much time we put into completing something. What matters is that we took the time to complete it.
57. Negativity is like eating bad fruit.
58. You can't lose what you never had, but you can gain what is to come to you.
59. Be blessed, it's a new day. Be blessed, God loves you.
60. You can do anything you put your mind to. Nothing is impossible. The word alone says it all.
61. You are not what the world thinks of you. You are what you think of yourself. So block out the negativity. Block out what people say about you. Block it out because all it does is take up space in your head. Instead, make room for positivity.
62. Your mood sets the tone for the kind of day you'll have. If we get up with a grateful heart, the day will go better. Listening or reading something encouraging and inspiring helps too.
63. If we want a better world, then it has to begin with us.
64. Nothing is impossible, and everything is possible.
65. Don't judge another soul, because he who judges is no better than another soul.
66. The ocean isn't too deep for you to swim, and the current isn't too strong to take you under. So when you think you are weak, then think of this.
67. Never give up on being the best you can possibly be.
68. Dreams do come true, so never stop dreaming.
69. Oftentimes we worry about something that is not even happening yet. Why worry about something that hasn't even taken place yet? We just cause ourselves more stress and worry when we do this. Just live in faith and not by sight.
70. Let faith take over everything.

I just want to conclude the ending of the book with a few more reminders that I have written about in my book.

A few ways to not be negative are the following:

- Love yourself.
- Be happy with your accomplishments.
- Look in the mirror daily and say, "God loves me. I'm a child of God. I'm awesome, smart, beautiful/ handsome. I have a lot to offer the world."

Go to church. Believe me this has helped me out in a big, big way. Get into the good word and read the Bible, pray, turn all your worries over to God, put it all in his hands. He gives us freedom to make our own choices. But what I do is have him lead me in the right direction and help me make all the right decisions. When in doubt, ask him before you do anything. He will guide you in the right direction.

Read something encouraging or even something that will help you drift into another world. Sometimes it is good to read something that is made up and not real.

I hope and pray all this helps.

Like I've said, I only give advice that works for me in hopes it will work for others.

I pray that this book touches your heart and that you will be ready to go live your life's journey. Amen.

About the Author

Jennifer Lyn Lupone is forty-five years old and lives in a small town called Oxford, Connecticut. This is the very first book that she has written.

She and her beautiful aunt live together with their cute puppy named Joey. She is five years old, but she will always be a puppy to them.

Jennifer's aunt has been like a mother figure to her ever since her mom went to be with the Lord in 1994.

She has an awesome boyfriend of three years. His name is Bobby St. John. He has five kids whom she adores.

She has been a hairstylist for ten years and loves what she does. She doesn't think she is the best hairstylist around. In fact, she loves seeing other hairstylists succeed.

Jennifer loves seeing others succeed and do good in life.

Her friends and family are her world.

Her motto is "God first, family second, and career third." Jennifer is honest, true, sincere, caring, bubbly, positive, outgoing, and more. She loves others and God